MY
PERSONAL
BRAND

A Guide for the
New Author or Soloist

Jennifer Lancaster

Power of Words

ISBN 978-0-9945105-8-7

Published by Power of Words, Australia.

Printed in Australia.

sales@powerofwords.com.au

NATIONAL LIBRARY OF AUSTRALIA

A catalogue record for this book is available from the National Library of Australia

A Reason to Read this Book

The new author or soloist often wants a better personal brand because they are trying to position themselves with more clarity and consistency. Their aim may be to launch new books and online programs. Is one of these cases you?

1. She wants to personally grow and move to a higher level, with more joy, more abundance, better clients, more income from different sources.
2. She wants to move away from all the confusion created by so much hype marketing online and focus on doing the two or three most important activities, easily fit into her work week.
3. He wants to establish the building blocks of personal brand and story so he can attract more people, sell more and be more successful.
4. Now a tired business owner, he wants to create online offers as a soloist so that he can semi-retire with an audience and leveraged form of income.

Contents

Preface

"Influence is best achieved through creating your personal brand…"
– Adam Houlahan, in *Influencer 2023*

Do you feel like all the content talking about being an author-preneur or large online persona isn't really talking about you? After all, you may not have the follower counts or the media interviews… the glamorous face or the famous connections. Then this book is for you.

Would you like to share more valuable opinions and write informative pieces on a relevant topic, but are not sure about it? Then this book is for you.

It's true that merely curating news content or posting quotes isn't enough to become a thought leader. Nevertheless, your opinions count, and your unique, personable self holds the key. Can you be yourself and talk about what you have found out?

If you keep this point in mind, I believe you can build a personal presence that stands out.

When looking at competitive titles for this book, I came across a book called *Solopreneur*. I had to laugh because this is what it said. "If you want to build a personal brand and establish yourself as an expert in your field, becoming a solopreneur can be a good option".

I don't get you, Jen. Well, who wants to simply become a 'solopreneur', i.e. a sole creator with too much to do? It's farcical. What many of us want is to have the *flexibility* of working for ourselves, the *leverage* of books, online courses or group programs, and the path to get that is… through the vulnerable route of curating your very own personal brand.

That's a powerful reason and the one that keeps me going despite a small number of followers. These aren't the only reasons to build a personal brand, though. Most solo consultants and coaches find that educating prospects on key insights and machinations within their industry (not just their offering) makes them much more attractive to those interested in mastering an area. Aligning themselves with a mission and other outward expressions of brand also helps greatly.

But before we get to personal branding, let's get your story straight.

1.

Why Storytelling?

Some of you will be coming from a corporation or business where there was a business brand. The brand itself might have an origin story, like that one of Dan Murphy's. But, it's a lot different when it's *you* that's telling the story of how you got started and why your lovely services and products exist. It may start to get a wee bit uncomfortable.

Most of us who are starting out with a blog or videos try to put a professional shine to everything. We want to create the most informative material, and we try to stuff everything possible into it! That's admirable, but I believe we need to share something that's higher up the 'who cares' ladder.

Tapping into our creativity, we must take ourselves temporarily out of our 'work worlds' to create riveting stories. So throw off that tie or high heel… and remember <u>what we have in common with others.</u>

A personal story that circles back to *why* you do what you do is one example. What happens though, is many very experienced and knowledgeable people encounter a blockage to sharing their raw and authentic story, the very thing that will connect them to others. The way to find out if you've got that block is to ask yourself some probing questions.

Do you believe in what you do? You probably do. But do you believe in <u>who you are and can be</u>? That you have a zone of genius? That one is far harder to achieve.

It may be because there are two voices inside us, not even including our mum's voice! Let's call them 'The Will' and 'The Worrier'. The Will wants to build a brand, go out and do talks, write a book or create a podcast, attract opportunity and money, and remain healthy while doing so. Sounds good. Problem is, when trying to do something new outside our comfort zone, we start to doubt ourselves. Like a monkey, the Worrier gets on our back and chatters in our head: 'you can't come up with a year of podcasts, plus you sound like gravel. Anyway, who's going to listen to them?'

Many of us seem to believe that others can do it better than us. We think they communicate clearer, sound better, look better, or write better. We may even believe that we are simply unimportant in the world at large. If you've ever thought *'who am I to....?'*, followed by whatever you contemplated attempting, then welcome to the imposter club, where nobody but ourselves keeps us playing small. (More on how to break through this later).

The fact that so many of us are feeling like an imposter when we step out to speak or write is, believe it or not, **a hidden asset**.

Acknowledging our inner chat, past problems, reluctance to change, a fear of judgment, or laughing about our procrastinating selves also draws us closer to others. Taking off your company hat and putting on your human hat will work for you, I promise.

Plus, it will help you start a distinctive personal brand... as you are being truly you, with your colourful background and unique set of colloquialisms.

Now let's get on with understanding the difference between organisational brand and personal brand.

Jennifer Lancaster

2.

Understand Personal Brand

"Small lights have a way of being seen in a dark world."

– Neal A. Maxwell.

What is a Brand?

Many people believe 'branding' is just something visual, like a logo or company signage and uniforms, but brand is much more than this. It encompasses an organisation's ethos, their graphics, their building, and the feeling it gives someone. It can encompass the values of the founder. Think about your favourite café-made coffee brand, e.g. Di Bella Coffee. It embodies the founder's commitment to service and quality.

Every successful company is built on a good brand: it's clear, consistent and easy to understand. Because of the faceless nature of corporations, many of them also need 'a personality': a spokesperson that embodies the brand. Cultivating a certain persona is what some famous founders do, which is usually reflected in their business too. Virgin's founder Richard Branson is really a confident introvert, one who likes to take risks.

To Personal Brand or Not?

Marketing messaging expert, Peter Sandeen, says that you can build your brand around one of three options. These are:

1. Yourself: For example, you're a great speaker that people relate to and trust easily, which makes them want to talk to you and follow your example.
2. Your company: For example, your company employs unusually experienced people from varied fields, which enables unusual service offers.
3. Your method/technology: For example, you've made an invention or created a unique process, which solves an issue unlike the solutions on the market.

Sandeen posits that which one is right for you depends on things like your future plans, e.g., selling the business or licensing the IP. A key consideration is differentiation; which of the three stands out most effectively.

What is a Personal Brand?

A personal brand is a cohesive identity that is associated with a person rather than a business. However, this identity can be used in a variety of ways, for example:

8

- to grow an actor or musician's presence without sacrificing their reputation
- to brand an author's look of their books, their blog and sales platform
- to give a blogger a look, quirkiness, ethos and colours that tie into their blogging aims.

Amy Green wrote in SmartCompany that personal branding is:

> *"How you are recognised and remembered.*
> *It is the art of bringing together your*
> *strengths, skills and your true essence, then*
> *implementing strategies to amplify your*
> *unique value to the world."*

So, a tad more than just a studio shot and a fancy piece of design then!

With an uncultivated presence, much of a personal brand is created from our own *personality*. Some people think they have to play this down, when in fact, it's much better to play it up. Think of how a larger-than-life personality and passion brought Steve Irwin and his respect for 'unlovable' animals to light. This was turned into a zoo brand (still featuring Irwin faces) and highlighted their projects.

With a managed presence, both personality and many other elements will create the impression that people receive and the authority created in their minds.

Parts of a Personal Brand

The parts of personal branding encompass:

- Your tone of voice – or the mood created
- Brand Promise
- Brand Personality / values
- Your skills and qualities
- The position of influence
- Distinctive Value Proposition

Think about how these apply to a personal brand. The first, tone of voice, is how you relate to others publicly (in all content/copy/books). This voice may put across a mood of a confidant, an expert guide, a quirky take, a controversial voice, etc.

Think more about what Brand You offers in the way of a *brand promise*. This is what your service or publishing imprint offers to fulfil, the fundamental elements. For example, my brand represents author growth and learning empowerment. Just doing it all and saying 'here you go' does not fulfil my brand promise.

Do you have a fundamental way of operating?

Up the energy

What type of energy is transmitted from the look, feel and words in your logo, website, and tagline? This should stem from your *'brand personality'*. Is it a bit bland sounding, with stock photos?

Pep it up a little by:

a) bringing your fun and informal voice to a distinctly dry industry, or

b) using vibrant video imagery with slogans, a philosophy or inspiring messages, or similar. (Ensure your slogan is focused on results).

Skills and qualities can be picked out to highlight judiciously. Although I have graphic design and email marketing skills, you won't hear me talk about them very often. They just aren't very relevant to my offering.

What *position* is your personal brand in the marketplace in terms of influence: hidden, becoming visible, or highly visible? There's a test you can do at Adam Houlahan's website that clues you into some common personality profile parts. This profiling system is based on the Wealth Dynamics system, which I enjoy too (I'm a Blaze energy and Creator/Star profile). Take the easy test at https://adamhoulahan.com/influencertest/

As we work more on our LinkedIn presence, guest articles and our public talks, our position of influence grows... as long as the work is focused on 'niche subject expertise'. Our visibility grows too. If I hadn't done this myself, I wouldn't be so sure. Plus, really, can so many smart people be doing all that work for nought?

Most importantly, what distinctive *value proposition* does your business offer? This should encompass emotional benefits, not just functional, since emotional benefits carry greater weight. *Ease of overwhelm from not knowing what to do* would be one emotional benefit.

Before a deep dive into these areas, let's go into some more blocks that people tend to have when putting themselves in the spotlight.

3.

Getting Past our Personal Blocks

You now know the foundations, so it's time for some self-assessment. This could be painful but bear with it. It really does get easier.

Tough questions to ask yourself:

- What habits are detracting from your goals, e.g. are you commenting on Facebook but not really marketing your own offers?
- What fires are you putting out in terms of clients or boss, while your own dreams die?
- How long do you spend worrying about something, rather than doing it?
- What is really the worst that could happen if you do experiment with a new personal online presence and bold banners?
- Conversely, what could happen if people like your new stuff and start contacting you, seeking your opinion or service?
- Are you charging (or earning) what you're worth?

These questions are meant to prompt you to think bigger, just like a private retreat... Just you, my words, and a notepad.

As introduced in the Storytelling chapter, those who are new to working under their personal brand feel at least a little fear and some have full-on Imposter Syndrome. I tended to worry about things like: *my course isn't good enough. That course creator is so much more tribe-attractive; my videos aren't smooth enough and with fancy backgrounds, my website isn't trendy or interesting looking. I don't give enough immensely unique value.*

Those thoughts were holding me back. These worries always stopped me from releasing or promoting past courses that would have helped earn income and grow my author brand. What I've learned is, an amateur attempt is better than nothing at all, as you can always improve the look of things as people enrol. Usually, they give feedback if they are enrolling at a free or discounted price. All feedback helps you to improve and effectively sets things as more balanced in your mind.

So, if your big intention is to create a course, then doing anything small, such as ordering the design of a course banner, is a concrete action towards that goal. It helps us believe that yes, we can make progress in something unfamiliar.

Scheduling in weekly time for your book or info-product creation and *marketing action plan* is important to progress. To make sure you do get things done, you might use a social media planner app, like Zoho Social, and set task reminders on your Google Calendar.

This type of habit is how online course creators get those larger goals achieved.

> *"As we let our light shine, we unconsciously*
> *give other people permission to do the same.*
> *As we are liberated from our own fear, our*
> *presence actually liberates others."*
> – Marianne Williamson

Be Aligned to your Intention

To build your self-confidence in this thought leadership stuff, you may need to change your outlook. Aligning your actions, remind yourself: **what is my intention?**

It's probably not simply to create the most perfect book or program... It's more likely to be: to *serve this group of people with a helpful book, course or program.* Or, *to give some key insights to interested people and inform their learning.*

One technique to get over this in-the-spotlight fear is to remember what your original position was and how far you've come, what you've learned. You probably do know more than you realise. And you are more than your job title, parenting role or business size.

You can also start small. Say it's speaking on social media that you want to do. Just start with 2-minute Facebook Lives or Instagram Reels on different subjects that have come up that week. Not everything has to be groomed to within an inch of its life.

Have that mastered? What about offering to talk to local business networks, chamber of commerce groups, and non-profits, with the reason to pay attention to what you say… e.g. how to avoid falling into scams, how to set up your computer correctly, or from dry accounting figures to fun and financial freedom. This is still small in scale but gives you the needed confidence to go bigger, say at national summits in your field or expos.

Writing also brings up our doubts about our talents and skills in this area. When I first started writing essays at TAFE many years ago, I felt like my writing was poor to middling, as those lines refused to flow. I could have stopped trying, saying to myself 'I'm just no good at this', which incidentally is a statement indicating a fixed mindset. Thankfully, a patient teacher got the red pen out and kindly helped improve the essay, allowing us students to rework the draft for a final, improved essay. I got a B. I worked *even harder* on essays in my Bachelor of Communications degree, where I proudly achieved a High Distinction for my essay on "using creativity in academic writing".

Writers are made, not born. There is no reason you can't improve your skills, especially with some mentoring help.

If you allow your subconscious/imagination to work on problems and barriers instead of shutting the doors with a fixed belief, then rough, unformed ideas will trickle out. Coupled with a strongly desired objective, like building something that helps the world, a creative and open mind can turn those rivulets of rough ideas into a raging torrent of visions.

With planning and dedication, these visions can be turned into strategies to meet that aim.

So, if you ever hear yourself saying, 'I'm not good at planning, organising, writing, etc…' rephrase it to be non-permanent and fixable, to be growth focused. For example, 'I've not been adept at organising my week, but now I have calendar blocking, I can use this tool to get better at it'.

You could also use *what if* technique. Like, what if I just write 500 words today on how I felt when starting out… and it doesn't matter how it comes out? Or, what if I simply create a title and concept for a course? I don't need to worry over who will buy it or invest hundreds of hours yet.

At this early stage, *what if* could mean you ask people in your business network for their feedback. If that concept is exciting to you and you share the idea in general with your closest business group, they won't shoot it down. They should in fact give you an idea of what they themselves want to know about it.

Share Your Plans

In fact, one way to create more momentum with this is to share your intention and plan with others.

When you share your plans publicly, you call in the consistency principle. The *consistency principle* states that 'people are motivated toward cognitive consistency and will change their attitudes, beliefs, perceptions and actions to achieve it'. Robert Cialdini wrote about how to use this principle to your advantage in his book *Influence, Science and Practice*. Basically, this means we feel deep-down that we must carry out plans we previously shared.

Sharing your plans publicly and having a mentor/buddy with a plan of yours is a sure-fire way to activate this principle. You can try to use it on yourself as well, by using self-affirming statements like, 'I am growing my skills in speaking', 'Image is one thing, but message is everything'.

This factor seems to be a big reason people want to hire a coach for their goals. It's helpful to be accountable to someone who is strong enough to call you out if you are dodging the work... or help you if you get stuck. These are the same reasons that beginner book writers want a writing coach.

4.

Actioning a Personal Brand, with the BREACH System

Imagine yourself back in 1920 and revelling in being the first business partner who educates (a coach). Just talking about the benefits of learning and developing a growing business would be enough to gain their curiosity. Now come back to today, 2023, when business coaches, trainers and strategists abound. Generic is no good; to stand out from others you will need to draw on your personality and values, your driving reason for doing this and your better world idea.

Purpose forms a large part. Going beyond the lifestyle wanted, what is the purpose of your work or creative works? What results are intended? Think about the benefits for others and why that matters. It may be so long since you thought of this that it's become a slippery eel idea. So catch that eel and write down why your work matters.

Your origin story plays a part here too, as it gives someone a feel for what got you started. Vulnerable and imperfect people often

Jennifer Lancaster

The BREACH System

Fearless marketing strategy
for the Author-preneur

Brand

Set up a personal brand for consistency,
with a brand board, values, main idea.
Make it like your personality.

Reach-outs

Message likeminded authors, partners
and prospects with a 3-step approach.

Energy

Bring personal energy and vibrancy to your
public life.

Authenticity

Personal brands must communicate with
authentic messages. Be you!

Charity

Fearless marketers find a charitable way to
make a difference through their
books/courses.

Host

Make your website your home base: for
podcast, challenges, blog, webinar, freebies.
Activate this web audience with personalised
education and calls to action

connect much better than those who are trying to be cast at a higher level, as perfect.

Introducing the BREACH System

When you've got a brand, you need to focus on intentionally putting out messages and vibes that constantly resonate. An acronym for this work helps us remember the key points. This one may have you thinking of a whale, perhaps an industry whale doing a beautiful thing called a BREACH.

Brand attributes. This is where we assess what our personal brand is saying, what our values will be, and set up a deliberate personal brand (with guidelines to follow). Colours, icons and typefaces are clarified, mood, professionalism or casualness of voice, and what you basically represent, e.g. caring about client results. This informs our personal mantra and our series of key messages.

Reach-outs. As we delve into in the Partnerships chapter, getting involved with campaigns through relating to others will push you further than standing alone. It's also a good deal cheaper than social media advertising.

Energy. We can't interest people by boring them with low mono-tones and ums. Whenever you are about to go on stage or camera, try to bring your personal energy up and remember the message to get across. Smile, toss that internal imposter aside, and laser focus that energy into the true value you're providing.

Authenticity. Some notable people don't cultivate a personal brand themselves. Ex-All Black rugby union star, Tana Umaga, leads from his values. In 2018 he stood down from the Head Coach role to help players one-on-one, passing on his experience and leaving his ego out of it.

Authenticity is important to everyone; so much so, it pays to think about how your real values and personality can shine in your pictures, articles, and videos. It is not about copying or grabbing at trendy words; authentic personal branding is about playing to your strengths.

> *Authentic personal branding*
> *is about playing to your*
> *strengths.*

Charity. Making a difference to the world is important to many of us. The trouble is, most of us don't know what to do to help! You could simply pick one charity to help, redirecting a set percentage of client profits or book profits to it. Aligning your work with something crazy important to you is the way to go.

Some ideas are:

- Merchandising ventures with charity brands (like *Love Your Sister)*
- Join *Kiva* – offer those in need micro loans – or pledge a percentage to any charity at *Buy1Give1.*
- Set up a t-shirt sales channel and give the money after the sale.

Charity efforts reflect on the wholeheartedness of your brand, personal or otherwise.

Hostess. Why do more people not secure their 'own name' website? It's a mistake I almost made myself, as it's all too easy to get carried away with 'book name' websites. Making your personal brand the web hostess will enable you to keep promoting books, courses, software, guides, journals and grow your following through a blog. Thankfully, my spouse secured my own name website domain, installed WordPress and a theme, and it grew from there.

While any old business 'hosts' a website, a primo personal 'hostess' also supplies free resources for others to enjoy, along with his or her own product line. Yes, a man can be a hostess too. So be the hostess with the mostess. For the domain suffix, you can choose from .au, .com.au, or .name.

Projecting your Brand, with Personality, Attributes and Values

Before you launch any brand awareness strategy, it would be wise to assess your traits, values, beliefs and what it shows others. Along with this, what abilities of people do you believe in? Do you have a real understanding of your clients and consumers? Their values?

After doing an Empathy Map, an exercise in client paradigm and what they think of you, I realised that there is no such thing as a typical author. There are many reasons to write a book and just as many reasons to build a personal brand. There are rich authors and ones in lack, expert ones and still learning ones. Reading past client testimonials, I could pick out not only key traits about me they liked, but also key problems they found solutions for. Just gold.

Cultivate an identity

No matter how big his business got, Gerry Harvey used his charisma and 'average Aussie' persona to connect with customers through the media, like radio. On a smaller scale to Gerry, Cat Matson has used personal brand savvy – and a giving spirit – to gain a sizeable following, both on social media and off. She also helps others 'Speak with Confidence' in her podcast and courses.

What kind of *identity* do you project? Do you naturally attract people and opportunity or do you prefer to hide behind the scenes? You might have to come out from behind the pot-plant at networking... because getting across your ethos and enthusiasm for your key message is going to work much better!

Rather than saying your occupation and that's that, you can help build your brand credibly by relating:

- Your personal principles and why you believe the philosophies behind your key messages
- The value you bring to your target market (see exercise)
- What others think of you in this space (client stories)

Try to integrate these into all of your marketing efforts, whether online or in person (at events). On the website, you could also list the successes you've had in your niche, e.g. a business award, a blog TopRank score, a high-level certification, or results of clients.

Stories about how you helped someone achieve or finish something is always the best advertising. The credibility of outsider 'social proof' is very powerful when it comes to target market attraction, so never forget to add testimonials to your website and ask for recommendations on LinkedIn, ask for endorsements on your new book, or mention new clients who achieved their goals in your introductory video spiel.

What are personal brand attributes?

These are the attributes taken from your personal self-assessment and considered friend's statements. Looking at various values and attributes of yours, you then decide which ones you'll bring out in public.

Choose up to five from the list below.

List of Core Values and Attributes

Achievement

Adaptability

Adventurous

Balance

Collaboration

Communication

Consciousness

Creativity

Curiosity

Diligence

Efficiency

Empathy

Empowering

Enthusiasm

Entrepreneurial

Environmental

Equality

Excellence

Financial Independence

Freedom

Frugality

Fun

Generosity

Guidance

Harmony

Honesty

Honour

Individuality

Innovation (personal)

Integrity

Justice

Kindness

Learning

Mastery

Personal Growth

Resiliency

Resourcefulness

Service

Self-reliance

Truth

Value-creation

Visionary

Did you have fun deliberating over these, going through your attributes and inner values? Is it hard to choose just those you want to put on public display? We have so many aspects to our personas, but those values that jump out at you and light you up are your ones. You might also note down a few ideas about how the minor attributes could be of value to others.

Many people will resonate with these same values: love, family, hope, humour, personal growth, passion, teamwork, service, integrity, openness. In fact, an outpouring of common values is key to the appeal of people like Anthony Robbins and Brendan Burchard.

People also react to a consistent message that relates to their own fallible traits. Comedians are expert at this. This alignment may even happen subconsciously.

Exercise: A brand and values assessment exercise is valuable. Answer these questions about external perception versus internal values/traits:

How does my personal brand currently portray me in terms of values?

How could I create an authentic vibe?

What usually puts people off in your world… e.g., is it blandness, is it fakery, is it hype?

What do they really want to know about my background and values?

This is where you grab a notebook and start writing, okay?

Now it's time to think about beliefs and life learnings.

Creating a Brand Story

Up till now, you may have been tempted to hide your personality in generic statements about excellence or dedication. The mistake I often saw as a copywriter was the company director being too afraid to talk about her history and specific values. But you must if you're to empathise with visitors.

In your story, try to take brave steps to reveal a failure – or something deep you discovered about yourself – and honestly state your position on a topic. Without this, you lose a magic opportunity to build rapport with your audience. Examples? We can look to Kate Toon's copy style, which is widely admired for sheer guts and wit and personality.

What do you believe in? I believe in a growth mindset: the ability to apply oneself to develop skills where one is weak. I also believe in the power of a creative mind: the ability to access deeper-level, innovative ideas when relaxing one's mind. Put those two concepts together – with a dash of critical thinking – and you can then approach all problems with an adaptable and open mind.

Strong beliefs like this, that are positive and portrayed well, can make for a strong personal brand ethos. Other people's euphemisms trotted out, do not.

Adding to your beliefs and ethos is personal motivations. Back to Wayne, a financial planner with a personal story to tell. Let's dissect it to polish up his raw brand story…

With financial planning, there is an extra layer of suspicion—some people even think they are just playing with others' money. So, advisors like Wayne need to share that they have come through the mud and learned to use money wisely. People like to see someone who has walked the difficult path and prospered. This introduction can be part of articles he writes as a thought leader.

Wayne wants to help others because a while back he went through a divorce and it took him some years to recover those financial losses. Would he just go out and complain about this? No! His whole brand story could stress the empathetic tone and involve the positive tip, 'use clever money management to get your life back', thereby putting a picture in someone's mind that they should pay down their mortgage fast, to get their life back (like he did). That it is not just 'nice to do'—it is imperative!

Once you have drafted your story, it's useful to keep this personal origin story in mind when writing your About page, blogs, introduction to videos, and first downloadable guide of 5-10 pages.

Another type of story is a turning point that may have led to your new passion for a non-profit, a signature program or an amazing course.

A turning point story has high stakes, it was important to your life. It has a degree of personal challenge and probably a degree of conflict. It can be very hard to see the connection between our own life challenges and our business, nevertheless, the people who come to you have their own blockages and challenges. These are often quite similar to what yours was.

And when you tell your story with the thought in mind to teach something—that someone will resonate with the sense of frustration, overwhelm, or other human frailty. We are all people, after all, not robots.

A turning point story makes a great Preface for a book, incidentally!

Exercise: Write out your personal brand story across at least five lines on a large notepad.

Messaging Tip: Generally, in the awareness phase of marketing messaging, the emphasis is more about your target individual and their goals rather than you and your goals. Keeping your own overarching purpose top of mind is very important though.

Find out the language of your clients or students, as they are probably saying the things that similar others want too. Some client reviews or recommendations will speak of your values, and there may be ones you've overlooked, so take a fresh look.

Creating a Point of Difference

There are many ways to stand out from others in business doing similar things. One way is to use creative messaging that resonates with consumers.

Mortgage broker Wayne has heaps of competition. He has a passion for not only getting the best home loan deal (a given) but also helping his clients understand the power of paying off their home loan faster. What one thing is Wayne really good at? He is awesome at putting charting technology to work to show inspiring outcomes. He also often thinks up ideas that his clients can use (e.g. Easy Tips to Pay Off Your Home Loan) which is useful for the blog.

So, he determines his point of difference: explaining the broader financial benefits of renewing home loans, with visual data. He could be safe about explaining this and keep it only to personal presentations. Or he could become:

Wayne Broker – showing you creative ways to pay down your mortgage faster and get your life back!

Emphasis on some personal traits and values, like helpfulness, honesty, wanting others to save, etc., could be stated in the background of this new business brand story. His photography would reflect his professional self in action.

A broker wants to offer many services but cannot highlight them all. By choosing a sector of the market to focus on (mortgage renewals), Wayne has a chance to attract the exact right customer who is motivated to get on track with larger repayments. A motivated customer who gets helped to their goals could also be a great advocate.

Together with the origin story, that's how business and personal brand differentiation can sit nicely together.

Personal strengths

Another element we can use is personal strengths. What strengths does Wayne display in his business? Perhaps he patiently explains new concepts carefully.

We can often find out our own strengths by reading our testimonials or feedback emails. Often, the same words keep coming out. These are obviously strengths, so if you spot them, write them down.

If you work with others, ask them what your strengths are. We often assume that everyone can do what we can, because the thing that comes the easiest to us is usually the thing that people come to us for. For example, clients don't come back to a psychology practice because it's the one the doctor recommended; they come because the psychologist listened well and got the client to change some perceptions.

One of these strengths, termed a 'superpower', is the thing that empowers you to be a one-of-a-kind in the marketplace. What is your superpower? It could be as simple as listening or clarifying; don't overlook the simplest strengths.

Exercise: Write out your desired personal brand voice and strengths ready for the public.

To reach the minds of your tribe, what kind of voice would you like to use? An authentic voice? A quirky voice? A controversial standpoint? (More on voice in *Personal Brand Guide*).

Jot down personal values others have noted. Add two of your core strengths you want to highlight, something of benefit to others.

Do New Customers Share Your Mission?

When we have products to sell, getting new leads is on our minds. However, asking a stranger to buy straight away is a little too forward. Most people need a little 'getting to know you' first and this requires many 'touch points', or places they see your brand.

That task is made a little easier when talking about something important: spreading a message of a better world, or at least a better lifestyle. You can give your personal and business brand a strong toehold in the market by inspiring through a larger mission. A customer-happy mission wins new people over with ease, and if altruistic, can even recruit a team of unpaid 'mission warriors' to spread the message.

A customer-happy mission is something people can get on board with, something that resonates with their personal values. It's not that people didn't care what your mission is; they just weren't able to grasp that it's an authentic pursuit of growth, people's happiness, health and success.

The mistake that companies often make with slogans and mission statements is making themselves the hero. Wrong. The customer or student is the hero and the business operator is their guide. (Kudos to *Building a Brand Story*, by Donald Miller).

A shared mission

Plenty of brands have created a culture of giving, all while they get people to know their wares. Australian companies like Thank You excel at this, with their inspiring change videos and novel ideas. Just by the way, they sold $10 million worth of product last year. They started with water and diversified to hand soap, pay-what-you-want books, sanitiser, etc.

Your mission doesn't have to be world changing... but are you thinking big enough? Large scope missions can help in the attraction and nurturing of customers. For example, design tool Canva launched in 2013 with a big mission of: "to empower everyone in the world to design anything and publish anywhere". This aim also drives improvements in the product suite.

Features of a business mission statement

I know what you're thinking: mission statements are cheesy. But this mission statement doesn't have to be crammed with corporate jargon; in fact, it should be driven by the 'big' reason you started out. You've no doubt read a lot of boring, hi-falutin mission statements so didn't want that for your public presence.

You probably also thought, 'people don't seem to care so I won't deliberate over it.'

A mission statement should be short, simple in language, include what you do and how you will deliver your vision. A business advisor, David Furze, once said, "Rather than by default, create a business by design … creating that strategy and purpose". 'By design' is what mission creation is about, not making up something with buzz words. It's also about involving the hearts and minds of other people.

Ideally, a mission will resonate with the values of people in the business, as well as their networked partners, followers and clients. It will become part of the ethos.

My business started off teaching self-publishing and book outlining, but Business Author Academy's new mission is 'to equip authors with how to create a rock-star online presence and profitable book/course'.

This mission arose because Australian authors who go to vanity/ hybrid publishers often fail to prosper. This fact leads to an important message: independent writers need an online presence and a path to market their wares if they are to make their creations financially viable. Always try to get at the genuine heart of the problem whenever creating a mission and vision.

How to create a slogan from the mission

If you've ever had trouble creating a business slogan, it may be because your mission and target market were not crystal clear. Once you know what the company does for people generally (the mission) and that it is bigger than egotistic goals, then it should be no trouble to make a slogan too. Although the difference is, slogans focus more on the customer benefits and strive to be memorable.

And remember, don't think about corporate phrases; think about human goals like personal growth, education, giving, creativity, togetherness, community, and similar themes.

In the book, *Book Yourself Solid*, Michael Port teaches soloists to be specific and clear in their language when creating a pitch or tagline. His advice is to put across part of your personality, as well as your positive vision for helping others, in the tagline. It is also about the emotional connection. His mission started with: I want to help people think bigger about who they are and what they offer the world. His tagline stemming from this became, "I'm the guy to call when you're tired of thinking small".

What values-driven mission statement could you determine for your business or book? Can you simplify it further?

Find Out What Your Tribe Cares About

Once you've distilled your company ethos into a mission and slogan, the next step is to communicate this mission to customers of a like mind. But it's not just an outward activity!

You start by looking at what kind of interests and worldview these people all share. This will help in marketing campaign planning, as well as bringing more authenticity to your website and any books.

36

Dan Kennedy called it the marketing triangle:

Take the right message to the right market using the right media.

He also taught to get ideal prospective customers to raise their hands and identify their willingness by requesting your free information, not on its own but through a multi-step sequence. This is direct response marketing in action.

Exercise: Go to SparkToro.com to put in your niche and find out what kind of podcasts your target audience listen to, what top websites they read, plus what #topics they care about. (Free sampling test or US$50 per month for demographics).

Also see 'Insights' in Settings if you have an active Instagram business account, to see the demographics of followers.

A mission shared with others is best for your business. So why not start to put your original and meaningful slogan in places like a business card, an introductory email, and in the footer of your website. You never know when someone will notice it and smile.

Jennifer Lancaster

5.

Steps to Publishing a Book

So, how does publishing a book reflect on our own brand?

Like me, you've probably been servicing clients and learning your trade for many years. Perhaps the reason you started this 'expert image' journey is because you wanted to stand out among competitors who do not have the same depth of knowledge or helpful experience.

Yet to continue the journey towards an effective personal brand … and a book as a calling card… takes even more dedication than usual. Some say they're too busy to write or speak, while others realise that credibility must be earned. In this knowledge age, we earn it through attention to detail and helpful information and advice.

My theory is that everyone who has been serving in their niche for ten years or more should delve into writing or speaking for their niche target audience. This is not a localised audience but an interest-based one.

This might involve, for starters:

- Creating an exciting online profile that relates to your target persona.

- Getting feedback on your appearance or head shots, and re-thinking it for the profession. (Personal stylists and photographers are cool people to use).

- Writing down all the questions new clients tend to ask you, so you have an arsenal of topics to write about.

- Listen to your audience first, reflect on what aspects you disagree with and then give your expert opinions based on your insider knowledge.

After these steps, you'll want to look at how you can put your 'verbal' advice into something written, perhaps starting with a niche blog, guest articles for magazines or business groups, and presentations. Or if you're ready for video, making short YouTube videos and lives which encompass your viewpoints.

Decide your Passion Angle

Some of us try to be too broad, trying to appeal across multiple markets with our first books. Big mistake! The most followed authors have a unique take on a topic and embrace an angle. One old example, Paul Smight (wrote Twitchiker) used his Twitter account to travel without money. Good thing was, Twitter is also easy to secure media attention if you have a decent size following (which he did). The angle worked with the topic AND the social media channel—a rare coup indeed!

Another example is Valerie Khoo, a believer in story, bold colours and artistic creation. She melded her love of story (as Sydney Writer's Centre leader) with bold creativity in her brand for *Power Stories* (2012) and a personal branded website. I noticed a few magazine articles she wrote for at the time and a cover shot of her at Switched On Leadership, signifying her publicity push during the book launch.

∾

Sometimes an author can grow beyond their personal brand and teach in a specific area worldwide, and there's nothing wrong with that. Emma Davies created *A Year with my Camera* to share her knowledge with amateur photographers, creating her first photography workbook. She built a group around it on Facebook. Then it started to feel like lots of effort with little engagement.

Emma loved the idea of building a community her own way, so she chose to create a Disciple app. Being a photography community, *A Year with my Camera* combined galleries and libraries, a forum and groups in a structured way. Through memberships or workshops, she has now helped over 70,000 students to unlock their creative potential. (Source: https://www.disciplemedia.com/case-studies/a-year-with-my-camera/)

Bear in mind that going through those hard early stages enabled her to reach that initial group of fans in the first place.

You can find inspiring creator stories at Thinkific, Kajabi and Skool as well.

Why Don't People Finish Writing a Book?

Before we delve into how to do these aspects, some major motivation is needed for this large workload of creating a book. Most newbie authorpreneurs are adamant they must hone their writing first (finding a voice) and do all this research. However, this belief may hold them back.

After interviewing New York Times' list bestselling authors, Brendon Burchard wrote that these authors never spoke about the idealism of being an author, or even about doing audience focus groups (research), and they weren't pegging all their hopes on getting a famous author to write a foreword.

According to them all, the five things that were important to authorship included:

1. Finish writing that book. Books in drawers don't do anything.

2. If wanting a publishing deal, get an agent. Otherwise self-publish.

3. Start blogging and posting to social media. Start an email list, as "email is everything".

4. Create a book promotion website and offer awesome bonuses to encourage lookers to buy the book.

5. Ask 5-10 partners that have large email lists to promote your book. (Of course, this will be reciprocated, especially when you've built up your list. Or sign them to be an affiliate.)[2]

NB. Getting a literary agent is American advice; some Australians win pitch proposals directly... if they already have an audience.

So Many Ways to Market Yourself with a Book

Besides having a major feeling of fulfillment from helping the world, there are many practical ways to benefit from publishing books. There is the placing of a Bit.ly link inside the book to a free audio download or quiz, to capture reader email addresses. But in addition to reaching new customers through the book-freebie and possibly teaching them something, there are other useful benefits of non-fiction book publishing.

Reading of the book helps the customer to learn more about your set of steps and ideas rather than drown in the overwhelming nature of online videos that pop up on YouTube. They feel closer to you as well, whether the book is personal story or 98% 'how to'.

You can't beat *national publicity* for both promoting a book and yourself, without spending any money. This should not cost lots of money though, as often you can deal directly with media newsrooms or editors. (See the one-pager book shot, on page 55).

You can go on niche subject *podcasts*, talking about the theories in your book and offering a sample chapter. You'll not only help sell a book or two but also pick up more email subscribers.

You can go on *television or radio*, talking about the problems these days closely relating to the theories in your book. Okay, this one is a bit harder, however, have you thought of doing video interviews with established YouTubers? They can get a lot of reach.

You can speak at *conferences*, talking more at length about one key answer. With a mutual arrangement, you might also sell your book to the conference organisers, to put into a goodie bag.

An alternative for those at home is to upload LinkedIn videos or audios, or YouTube/Facebook Lives, as part of a multi-channel strategy. Virtual Summit appearances are also a possibility once you have a slide presentation locked down and rehearsed. Mention your book in the bio and on the last slide page.

You can use your book as a base to create social media content for 52 weeks. You might create one interesting quote a week from the book or its theme and use an automated tool to put it on social platforms for you.

If you don't want to pay for social media schedulers, you can simply use Canva Pro to schedule these visual posts, and post text ones straight to LinkedIn. Canva Pro or Team is paid monthly or annually. Virtual Assistants can alternatively run the content system if you're too busy.

You can also use your printed book as a calling card when you have an in-person meeting. If done professionally and targeted right, it's better than a sales brochure.

Even if 'nobody reads these days' (some say), your book will NOT be thrown away. In fact, people don't even have to read it all for it to give the author credibility in that area. As Andrew Griffiths told the room at an event, one boat vendor wrote a book on how to run and enjoy a family boat and this led to better boat sales. They picked up the book and were sold on the benefits of boats, leading naturally on to being sold on buying a boat from its author.

To do this, use a sophisticated email marketing system or course platform website builder. Most paid ones allow use of your own sub-domain name, and landing and thank-you pages are simple to build.

Let's go into this a bit deeper.

Elements of a Book Funnel Offer

You can sell the book at wholesale cost on a simple book landing page, including print and postage. The next page after the purchase is your personal video with a bonus free offer. A one-hour webinar could be offered on this Bonus web page. This is a longer-term approach, has more steps, and usually contains a high-level program offer.

After you offer your segmented audience exciting and tailored niche content for free, immediately focus on getting a course or program together to take them deeper. We tend to underestimate the demand for deeper content. Things like online video training, in-person workshops, group sessions centred on a goal and the like are very sought-after in some areas. Think of the people following Alex Hormosi, all hoping like heck to be able to earn $3 million a year so they can join his elite mastermind.

You might offer a next-level training program just after purchase of the book (whether they buy direct from your website at full price or through an ad with a discounted price). Internet Marketers term this a *one-click upsell*.

This strategy could become your best friend if you ever go into publishing and selling directly online, and phase out one-to-one consulting or coaching. (See #3 in this article: **https://www.clickfunnels.com/blog/one-click-upsell/**)

However, the majority of established authority authors are content to offer a signature training program to email subscribers and book purchasers, about a month later. This is a good amount of time to have read the book and is not reliant so much on the buy button trigger-finger. Remember that half your audience will not have read past chapter one because life got in the way.

Making a book purchase all part of consulting, coaching services or course is quite the eye-opener, when you realise how many authority authors aren't utilising it and instead rely on Amazon royalties. This means getting 70% of ebook retail and 60% of print retail, minus the not insignificant print costs. (Cough, splutter at that thought).

Emails welcoming your new book readers is important here. A series of six emails could be set up in your email marketing system (which carries an unsubscribe link) to let them gain an insight into what journey you've had in becoming an author, the kinds of topics they can expect, to ask a question, or share your stance on something relatable.

A welcome series is for gaining trust, so don't send emails saying, "my website just launched". Rather, include mention of your blog or upcoming book in a later newsletter about the topic.

Before getting overwhelmed with all this, remember that it's your vision for what you want to do with your thought leadership. Stepping into the spotlight is necessary when you create a book, so if you don't want this at all, then don't put a book out.

Building an Author Platform

When asking new authors when they think it would be time to build their author platform aka online presence, this is typically what they said:

"I will focus on that when I've finished my final draft"

"I will start planning the marketing when I've got my book cover and edits done"

"I am in creative mode now, so I will worry about that when I am launching".

In other words, they are putting off till tomorrow what they could (and probably should) be doing NOW.

Admittedly, it might help to have named your book title and come up with the angle (explained in just a bit) – that is always going to help. But you don't need to wait... since notoriety as an author never happens overnight. It is a long, slow road, best taken one pitch, tweet, or post at a time.

Definition: An angle is a way to verbalise a gap in the market, whereas a hook is a pithy sentence which intrigues with its question or promise. No angle and no hook = low sales

Looking good, with brand imagery

If you write for business purposes, the colours and the angle of the book or program sold is all part of the brand. I stumbled on this when I got a superbly designed cover for Power Marketing, thanks to my designer spouse, with a website and bookmark to match.

My book's bright blue and gold complementary colours were carried on, past the book, to the Power of Words business look online. There were even a couple of people who simply LOOKED at the cover and title and asked me if I was a marketing consultant. That is the power of a well-designed cover!

Sure, a good designer could come up with ideas to suit you, but it's more likely that you will give direction on preferred colours, colour tone (muted or bright?), serif or sans serif typeface (i.e. classic or modern type), and overall image you want to put across.

These elements go into your **personal brand style guide**:

- Brand colours in CMYK, for print, and HEX codes, which are for websites (two or two plus a muted colour)
- Logo in three different ways. Square, rectangular, and reversed out.*
- Typefaces and fonts
- Slogans
- Tone of voice example (whimsical or strident; wacky humour or helpful)

* You may prefer to use a publishing imprint logo. Reversed out means, for instance, the logo could be white on black in some cases. Transparent background logos can also be of use, to put onto web banners.

The personal brand guide created can then flow to author headshots, author website look, brand values, and more.

Brand colours:

Set up your author brand colours (two is good), theme ('saving money' is mine). Working with a designer will help to ensure your brand is awesome, from the typeface chosen down to the relevant logo for your imprint.

Remember that you'll need to have photos with a book cover later (which will contain your colours), although these can be photo-edited later if the initial photographs include you holding up a blank book.

Tone of voice:

What does your written tone of voice say about you? If you usually have someone else write for you and don't deliberately give examples of tone of voice, your personal brand may be muted. It takes a delicate touch to edit copy and keep the writer's voice. Similarly, to write conversational copy takes some knowledge of that person's personality.

So, one answer is, for personal introductions such as your LinkedIn summary, write it yourself using your natural voice (perhaps record it first if you're not a conversational writer), then get a brilliant copy editor to check that it's grammatical and consistent. Later, you could show this piece to any copywriter you hire, for her to get a feel for the written voice. Keep this energy alive in your home page and 'about me' web page.

Pitch:

You need to get your media pitch ready. Firstly, what timely/newsworthy hook might you create? Secondly, summarise what your book is about.

Example Hook: Isn't it crazy how Australians get scammed more than $21 million a year when they really want to invest for wealth?

Example Pitch: My new book, Creative Ways with Money, helps people understand how past scammers have operated and explains how your mind's greed and fear blocks your investing success.

Handily, this can also go into your media/book kit, a PDF with blurb, head shot, mini bio and your social media handles.

Reach the whole world easily, with Print on Demand

You can, with some good production values, get your book out to the world cheaply. (It's the editing, marketing and design that costs the money). If you don't title your book as Australian and you do some promotions that reach globally (e.g., being an expert guest on a US podcast), your book will probably get some credence and be sought from lots of places you'd never expect. You do not have to print overseas or be represented at book fairs in Germany to do this.

IngramSpark tend towards professionals more than Amazon KDP, also with higher proof costs. This Print on Demand makes it a little easier to work with our Library Suppliers, who are called ALS, Peter Pal, Southern Library Supplies, and Raeco Library Solutions. Correctly filling ISBNs are also important to slightly better book discoverability.

When you publish with distribution to Global Connect and fill out the relevant pricing, you can let your book go to other markets, like Canada, US, UK, and Europe, plus all countries aligned with Global Connect: Spain, India, China, etc. You may need an ABN to join.

When you do the production yourself, you must buy about 10 ISBNs (as you need one for each format) and pay a new publisher fee at Thorpe-Bowker (MyIdentifiers.com.au).

IngramSpark has print facilities in the UK and Australia in addition to the United States.

To be honest, there are barriers which prevent retail sales in traditional bookshops. Traditional publishers can work the numbers by printing bulk quantities cheaply, have distributors who will do the sales legwork, and still have a profit if those big numbers mainly sell. Indie publishers don't have the pull with retail distributors and cannot risk large amounts on printing books in bulk for consignment.

Yet the alternative of print on demand is inherently flawed for wide sales. For instance, with IngramSpark, the usual split to wholesalers is 55% of RRP to them and you pay for print, though this is a little flexible. Apparently, though it is publicly unspoken, Ingram distributors take another 20% on top, leaving high street bookstores not quite so amenable.

The only answer for the business-minded brand builder is to advertise your new book (author bulk order) using videos or ads, a landing page, and capture the buyer's email addresses. Capturing the email in a creative way is certainly a plus, because you probably have more lucrative things to promote later. One big advantage of doing this is control of prices and direct promotion, which you won't have with global distribution.

The other secret is to only buy in what you can reasonably sell. Don't let ego rule the size of your orders; think instead with your calculator!

This means don't focus so much on the highest royalty, focus on what potential line of learning products you could offer after the person reads the book. (More on this in 'Book Funnel').

With the print order calculator, make sure you know what the print costs will be and whether the retail price would cover printing, two lots of shipping, and a small portion for book design and editing fees.

Produce a paperback

Your book must represent the highest quality that you can muster. It's representing your talent and so must be edited and formatted properly.

Editing books was a big part of my work life, and I do it by listening to the words as well as minding grammar rules. If you can't listen to your words and find missing words, then it's not a job for you. Luckily, there are lots of editors with 10+ years of experience in editing nonfiction. You could use American, English or Australian editors of nonfiction, bearing in mind that quality can be vastly diverse anyway.

Beautifully simple covers create a desire to click on to read more, while busy, ugly ones detract and repel. Internal book typesetting is also important; designers can match internal fonts to the typeface on the cover and add flourishes (called Printers Ornaments) to add additional style. Always ask to see samples and don't just buy dead dull templates!

Furthermore, never rely on a subsidy press package offer to provide your book with a cover; source a book designer yourself through LinkedIn or finding the designer's name inside the imprint page in Australian books you own.

Going to print, a paperback book will need 300 DPI, so any photos or illustrations will not be the same as website photos. Pictures also need to be in CMYK, which colour make-up ties to the four-colour process that printers use, rather than RGB format, which is what screens use.

Proofs are necessary, which is a sample copy delivered to your door and ordered well before 'distribution date'. Private printers charge $30-60 more for these than do print on demand. A POD proof costs about $25 with shipping.

Promote:

Promotion isn't just plugging your book on launch. It's doing a host of activities that relate to you as a writer (rather than just personal). So set up your 2-4 social media profiles to say 'author' and reflect this theme and brand. Some, such as YouTube, have very wide banners that you may need a designer hand to create.

The articles (or essays) you write to promote your discoveries, your theories, and your research will all help to create a desire for a longer piece – your upcoming book. Some magazines will pay for quality submissions of a certain length.

Then on launch, you can start sharing an excerpt of the book with relevant magazines, journals and so on. It's best if these are offline but it could be good to hit up high-trafficked sites. You can check article-share numbers by searching on https://BuzzSumo.com/content-research for your topic specifically.

Many authors build their social media followings by being influential in multiple ways in the world of business, consulting or coaching. Few have 'instant luck', announcing they're going on some sort of mission and get the media limelight.

If every media pitch fails, you can always post articles direct to LinkedIn and share with your network. But don't give up at the first 'no response' – it pays to ask more questions and get in touch in a new way (tweet / message / phone call). Journalists' and editors' email inbox are overflowing with news, and so a new article pitch or release often gets missed.

Follow-ups are always key in news media and blogger attraction.

One-Sheet Book Shot

Created with Canva or Indesign, the idea is you put all the data from your finished book on this one-pager, include the sales blurb, and send it to various online media. (The simple pitch may work better for a story in mass media).

Here are the parts to remember to include:

- Blurb – 100 words
- Author and book cover shot
- Very short bio (include country)

- Prices, formats, publisher, ISBN (important)
- Where to buy the book or eBook from.

Learning What *Not* to Do

You can also learn a lot from amateur authors with no brand knowhow. An extremely talented and funny legal niche writer in Australia had the books, the background and business, but not the branding sorted. Every cover had a different font. The eBooks contained interesting cartoons and made all valid points, nothing wrong there, but I feel the price was wrong and most books had no Amazon reviews.

However, they had some good editorial reviews (put in via Amazon Author Central). The About the Author section was too long and not really focused on what the reader needed to know. He could always add the funny bits once the important parts were covered off.

Some other mistakes were made. On one book, the book title read differently to the cover art. They must be the same. Sometimes the cover cartoons were too small to understand in miniature, such as when shown in the recommended books list. One or two cover images were puzzling as to why they belonged with the book – there was a mismatch between the meaning of the title and image. The titles were sometimes all uppercase and sometimes upper-and-lower. One title was unreadable due to the shadow treatment.

The desires of the reader were alluded to somewhere, but not really a factor in the blurbs. **Most bestselling how-to books focus largely on the reader's goals and how this book meets them.**

Critiquing is easy, but we all start out with learning bumps. My own books have also suffered from inconsistent production across time, with different cover designs and few reviews, so I am not preaching from a high castle.

Studying authors who do have a vibrant, consistent branding approach will teach you more about it.

Here are the lessons from the above mistakes:

- Ensure all the typefaces are similar; at least maintain sans serif (block type) or serif, all caps or upper/lower case. Plus not too squashed up.

- Ensure the reader is the main focus of the blurb, not the author.

- Ensure the image used is in sync with the title and book promise and is clear.

- The tone of voice is on the same level as the topic's content and is likely to resonate with its reader group.

- Focus the last line of the blurb on what value you're offering the community.

Once again, aligning to our target audience's values is an important factor. The more they identify with your values and aims, the more likely they are to buy something from you and listen to what

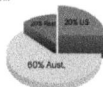

Sample Media Kit adapted from Canva

you have to say. But, if you disregard this and never tell anyone your values and personal background that's relatable, they don't have any basis for following you online.

Photo Ready

One way to solidify a personal brand image is through amazing photography (of you and your books or products). The higher up the online influencer tree you go, the more you need to wow with bespoke photos and close-ups of yourself speaking, book signing, or coaching clients.

Getting some pro photos done myself, by Leoni Bolt, it was remarkable how much better they were than 'shots at home'. Even though I was unsure if it was all just a silly idea, these photos made all the web and print paraphernalia look smart.

Colour-matched photography means the clothes you wear or background exactly matches one or both of your brand colours. Bold block colours (no patterns) work best, against white, black or grey pieces. As long as you own it, any colour you love that gels with the image, gets a big yes!

Local examples:

- Michelle O'Hara (Marketing) – resplendent in yellow jacket with black

- Trish Springsteen (Authoring) – royal purple, from hair colour to jackets

There are top-level brand photographers who specialise in drawing in these colours when doing a photo shoot.

Tip! If you're in the creative services industry, a web-based portfolio is a godsend because when you pitch for work, you can link back to it. Behance offers a free portfolio page.

Design Tips for Media Kit Layout

For more gravitas than just a book one-sheet, you may want to create a 3-4 page PDF to easily share. This design is usually based on a media kit template, for ease of design.

Choose two typefaces, which match each other in weight (using sans and sans serif is fine). Go for 11 or 12 point if in doubt about body font size. Give the images a bit of room. For a longer kit, include more media-oriented pics, such as you doing a talk.

While it may be difficult to get going with media publicity for an upcoming book launch, if you take a simple step like creating your author media kit, it may propel you to do more media interviews. And that's a good thing!

———

Creating Media Kits in Adobe InDesign

If you use InDesign, you can download a free 'blogger' media kit template from Adobe and change it, as I did. You may not have the fonts, so just replace with fonts you do have. Just ensure they have bold and effective headings.

———

The Author Media Kit Checklist

Here is a guideline for an author who has a blog and business.

- ☑ Short Bio (about you section, including any related awards)
- ☑ You with Book Photo
- ☑ Listener/reader offers, including any discounts
- ☑ Book Cover, Title, and Price
- ☑ Overview of what your book or product is about
- ☑ Questions they could ask you
- ☑ Main social media account names (if good, all follower numbers)
- ☑ Author Website URL / Blog URL / Podcast name/app

☑ Topics on blog (unless general) and 1-2 images

☑ Past articles you've written or media collaborations you've done

☑ Other Book Titles and Your Services (if related)

Bonus material:

Download a free sample Author Media Kit here:

https://jenniferlancaster.com.au/marketing-and-copywriting/publicity/media-kit-template-free/

~

In summary, you'll want to identify your values, personal strengths, point of difference, and hook to carry over to a book or program. Then consider your chosen predominant colours, tone of voice, and photography, and think about making these tie in. All this makes up your personal brand.

Reinforcing this brand across your social media presences, website and personal appearances (e.g., a roll-up banner) will make for a consistent approach and a trustworthy presentation.

Jennifer Lancaster

6.

The Five W's of Marketing

Most people start out trying to market themselves with a bunch of tactics. It's far better to start with a well-crafted strategy, so first comes the crucial planning steps. I call it the Who, Where, What and Why. This information will dictate your marketing plan.

To guide your work, use your unique Personal Brand Guide, which is a small document to keep handy on your desktop.

You must do research to find out what is on people's minds in your area. What are their fears, desires and questions?

See **Answerthepublic.com** for searched questions, Google Suggest and Amazon Suggest for suggested trending keywords (shown as you type or further down), and use **SparkToro.com** to research the audience's media habits/hashtags. Prepare to be amazed.

On Answer the Public, I found out that 1,200 people monthly search for the term "personal brand" – which netted about 30 related questions. Food for thought as I created this book.

WHO

Every marketing plan starts with the group (or segments: marketing jargon) of people you want to reach. There are all different things to consider, like:

Demographics – M/F, age, income, stage of life.

Psychographics – what they have in common interest-wise, e.g., business growth readers, self-development junkies, graphic designers, etc. A very important part to consider.

Benefit sought – perhaps a mix of people that all seek the same specific outcome.

It's good to consider each in turn. Don't be like the telemarketers who say, "I can get you first page on Google!" when they don't even know if you have the desire to yet. Really find out *what people want to know* and their objections to buying what you do.

So, pick two Personas that represent this nice mix and find a person that matches each from all the people you know. We'll call these A and B, although they could get creative names that match. In my Creative Ways with Money book, I picked: A) Aussie adults who enjoy new creative ideas, and B) those who are likely to be interested in fixing their poor investing (scam-ridden) past.

I talked to each of these while writing my book, as I know both personas' mindsets.

WHERE

These groups of people read stuff and look at images, videos or blogs online. Putting aside your distaste for certain social media types, where does (Persona A or B) usually hang out? Could you find out by doing research with SparkToro?

Facebook and Instagram Ads help by offering interest-based marketing or geographic based or similar audiences to yours. Do these ads reflect your genuine voice (written or spoken) and ethos? It's better to stand out while resonating with a niche group than blend in. Also, don't be prey to Meta's cunning ploys to part you with money before you're quite ready to advertise.

Instagram (organic) is more for 'showing' what you do, creating an insight into what you do in your work and life. It is optional for B2B. *Facebook* is for connecting with similar others, and joining interest groups is the way to do this. No point in wasting your time by posting to your page, but you should ensure your Facebook personal profile has a touch of your professional or creative work in the banner and bio, as people will check this out.

Search engine listings are the place for geographic-based service or product finders, but be aware that books and knowledge graphs about people (authors) come up too. All sorts of things are shown which vary on the type of search, e.g. recipes, tweets, video tutorials, and lists. When designing for this it is called structured data.

Google My Business is for the local listing of your business, which is optional if you work from home. If you have an online store, you can also list items via Google Shopping, with or without advertising. Items can be books or workbooks that you post out. It is not intended for digital or services.

The other kinds of 'where' that are often forgotten are in-person and direct mail.

In-person talks means planning the same interesting presentation to a number of groups or virtual events, with your books available. That way, only one set of work is needed. This is quite different to public speaking for pay, which is often tailored to the event. The clear advantage of in-person talks is the trust-building is easier. Don't worry, any mistakes can be quickly covered by making a joke. Remember to explain concepts slowly and clearly and introduce what you stand for and why.

Direct mail is for special offers of your authority-type book, workbook or perhaps a fun competition and is easiest to your vocational association or customer list, since you can get their address. This allows you to follow a mailing with more promotions or nurturing. Bear in mind that people need to be willing to type in a website address to sign up for the item. That said, it is also possible to offer a mail-in coupon with a stamped envelope.

Cultivating media presences

I cannot emphasise enough the power of media coverage to boost your personal brand. This media buzz doesn't stand alone though; it can form part of your book marketing and thought leadership 'funnel'. Make it super easy for their audience to both find your online presence (e.g., your website or LinkTree page) and understand what you offer for free.

There are many interest-based magazines you can become a writer for (temporarily). With a broader audience, such as women in mid-career, you may need to take out any jargon as there will be a broad cross-section.

There are also online media sites you can write for. What kind of audience do they have? How many actual readers? How much might it cost to reach that audience, or alternatively, will they perhaps pay you? Don't fall into paying richly for placement in spurious magazines to promote yourself.

If you do some research, you may find higher-level and niche places where you write for free but get a very nice article and byline. If you can include a backlink, some reputable magazines will allow this 'follow' link to help your own SEO (search engine optimisation). You could check with **KeywordsEverywhere.com** what Domain Authority their website is. (This is a very low-cost extension for Chrome). My advice is to link back from websites with over 20 DA.

Finding relevant places to write for is easy. Use this Google search term if seeking, for example, female founder magazines in Australia: Female Founders {key term} "write for" .au. You can also use ChatGPT to find more international article sites to write for by being specific like this.

As time is limited, ensure you are getting the word out in places where people will be most interested in your message.

WHAT MEDIA

What media are you using? Choices range from social media quotes (Twitter/FB/Insta), to news media outreach, to blog posting and guest blogging, to raffles, to photographic flat-lays (for Instagram).

Whatever you decide on, think about the REACH of the media. Respected media strategist, Michelle Fleming, prompts us to consider the cost per one-thousand impressions – or CPM – to help contrast various media choices for advertising.

Also think about your preferred talent and skill when choosing the media type, e.g., some people are great at photography whereas others are better at writing articles.

If it's a message for consumers, make the book press release more of a news article. Editors are busy and want to get interesting material. Write the article telling people a warning, give some specific tips, or write about how you can get your loved one to do the dishes and rub your feet! Whatever is related. Put about where you can find your book (or service, if relevant) and your name and credibility strap-line in the bottom line.

A *credibility strap-line* is a byline that tells people why you're the 'go to' expert. If you're light on the formal achievements, allude to the personal growth path you've been on since a big event in your life, or similar. E.g. After falling for a scam, Jennifer writes books to explain how others can put their financial house in order.

WHY

Go back to your personal mission and values. Missions about health, education or relationships can seem broad, so it's time to get specific. Determine real goals that people will resonate with.

If you want to rid the world of nuisance callers, then say so!

If you love to give to kids and volunteer at school while writing a children's book, then say "I give time to our school community so school students are cherished" and other things along those lines.

The *reason why* is important when there is so much noise out there. How many unimportant things do you see on Instagram, when there are so many real issues to address? Putting your causes and values in your marketing helps to build a like-minded audience.

We also need reasons to get out there. Authors and business owners alike often lag on regular marketing activity, so how can a motivational reason help? Coming from a bigger 'why' perspective, it gives any leader a strong enough motive to move past their comfort zones.

Some other benefits are:

- Rather than worrying over your 'product' (book or service), your message is front and centre. This is great because it means people connect with your hook and your ethos.

- You will be learning about brand, benefit writing, landing pages, keywords, and teaser lines: all stuff that is handy for attracting anyone to any meaningful book.

WHAT MESSAGE?

A **niche marketing** mindset is needed in line with message writing. That's because choosing a niche will help an author attract fans with a laser focus. Using a certain phrase, a slogan or even a book title that shakes things up can be an 'attractor factor', e.g. 'Joyful Eating' or 'The Subtle Art of Not Giving a F#$$'.

> *"The mistake a lot of people make is flip-flopping around a niche.*
>
> *The less niche you are, the bigger the audience you're going to need to support it.*
>
> *The more niche you are, the more you're going to cut through the noise and speak to your ideal customer."* – Bob Gentle, from Amplify.me

5 Key Messages

Defining your marketing messages comes *after* the work done in Chapter 1, not before. Work up a few ideas from these bases:

- Select 3 values, leading to your 'mantra' – which is crafted in a way to remember it

- Beliefs behind the mantra

- Why this subset of consumers should perk up their ears. It has to be life-changing (better health, sound sleep, wealth, more business leads, creative expansion, new relationship, allowing abundance, etc). After all, nobody ever signed up to a course or signature program to just learn a few things.

Let's start with some for a new book & course marketing program... starting with my chosen values of *creativity, fun, empathy*.

> Mantra: 'Make marketing fun and never work a day in your life.'

> Other messages: Marketing and monetizing a book doesn't need to be so hard. It can be creative.

> Authors need more lucrative income sources, not just books.

> Is it time to leave the rat race... and join the online publishers game?

> Q. Won't making a course and lead funnel be painfully slow and hard?
> A. No, it can be done in 90 days when you've got support.

While making the messages, try to choose words that either disrupt what's expected or play with words that are said in their mind but never usually said out loud. Salespeople call these objections. If you write a message and feel that you've heard this before somewhere, erase it and try again.

You might be tempted into giving your power over to generative text AI, but here is what Simon Kingsnorth, CEO of SK said about this:

> *"ChatGPT can be a game-changer for businesses looking to inform and refine their brand strategy, speeding up the process of content planning, competitor analysis and much more. However, always supplement it with real-world data, critical analysis, and your own creativity."*

Exercise:

Write five key messages. You could make one of them a promise, with a timeframe the result will be done in and a beneficial goal. Know the end pain/problem you solve for customers. Think not in terms of 'tax returns fast' but rather 'no tax headaches this tax time, and a better return to boot'.

7.

The Personalised Funnel

The *Book Creation Success* program was ready and waiting, two years in the making, but Facebook ads sent directly to the landing page were *not* converting. I tried promoting a free call option. Nada. Freebie guide personally offered? A couple of local contacts opted in to get my guide. Then I tried automating LinkedIn invites and added 100 new contacts with some nice prose on the invites. But I still didn't get a bite on the free call offer. (Not a great idea).

You might have found yourself in similar confusing circumstances, so what do you do?

Nothing beats personalised messaging. Without forethought, I checked out a contact's personal LinkedIn profile and it was apparent that she was under-selling her years of teaching experience. I figured I'd just help out, with a friendly sandwich of quick tip, ask how she was doing, and chat about what I have been doing.

Next, I sent her (via LinkedIn message) a free 'cheat sheet' on writing an author bio, from my older marketing course, which I freely admitted that was done a while back. Lo and behold, she came back with, "This is exactly what I'm looking for. Can I enrol?"

Besides being easy and natural to do, assessing people's needs and giving first is now a part of my audience building toolkit.

This path of giving first and waiting for it to be the right time for them is a great way to sell something like specialist education. It requires very little 'push marketing'.

They have to believe first, that:

1. You are an expert in this field
2. You are genuine and helpful
3. The offer is ideal for their level of knowledge and main objective.

Putting the Personal Brand into Profit

Did you know that the reasons people like Neil Patel sell their courses at $1,000 is so they can advertise, get less troublesome students, and create more profit…? That said, Neil Patel and James Tucker can probably ask this price because of their personal brand name value, AKA their 'street cred'.

It is darned amazing to consider the value that Neil Patel has built up for himself, from ordinary London roots. An entrepreneur at heart, he's 36 and worth a reputed $30 million. He is the founder of Crazy Egg, Hello Bar, for a time part of Kissmetrics (2008), and wrote the marketing blog, Quicksprout.

In 2014, Neil and partner Hiten Shah left Kissmetrics and took on a challenge to get 100,000+ visitors to his personal blog. They ran several tests, including for mere mentions of his own name and how this might affect Google page rankings and hits. It did! (Source: OBpedia.com, Angelsandentrepreneurs.com)

Now, the Neil Patel blog receives millions of visitors a month who want to grow their business with digital marketing (preferably the inexpensive way, with content). Even though his blog mentions "I wish I didn't start a personal brand", keep your tongue in cheek since it mentions the 3-4 x growth his personal brand name enjoyed in 5 years, not to mention the flow-on effect to his blog's page ranking and visits.

Fundamental elements to this growth were:

o Blogging consistently for a decade, publishing 4,868 posts on NeilPatel.com.
o Daily podcast (Marketing School) with his partner
o Weekly video content – YouTube (650+ videos) and Facebook Live, LinkedIn.
o Prior, Neil guest posted weekly (1,831) and spoke at conferences (50 a year for a while)
o The Neil Patel blog has been translated into four languages, and more.
o Neil paid to create the helpful tools Ubersuggest and Subscribers, along with many free courses on marketing.

Did you notice the crazy numbers? Besides being prolific and having a team, the key to the Neil Patel success story is his focus on giving wholeheartedly all the details on what people want to know, for free, and providing tools too. His generosity also has calls to action of course, but it's interesting to note that you don't have to be communicating at genius level to attract the masses. Simple is best.

Neil's colour is orange and his face is everywhere.

On his blog, he points out that the downside to growing such a wildly successful personal brand is the difficulty in keeping the legacy going, in sickness or even death. The face of the brand has to be in the public eye (on videos) and it's also harder to sell a company named after someone if people are used to their presence.

Being the Purple Cow is Just the Start

Here are some great tips from Peter Sandeen. (Petersandeen.com)

1: It's not enough to be different; your target customers have to see it as unusual and actually care about it. Even if you know something is first to market and highly impactful, your target customers might expect to get something similar from elsewhere.

2: Potential customers don't compare you only to your direct competitors; they also consider other solutions to these same problems. Even if you have no direct competitors, people might compare your solution to multiple other options. Perhaps a book compared to a course.

Differentiation (finding your Unique Selling Proposition) can be quite difficult to do.

> *"It can be frustratingly difficult to find the right differentiators to build your own marketing around. You might easily see what differentiates others, however, seeing your own business from the perspective of a potential customer is often the most difficult part of growing your business. So, don't judge yourself when it's not clear to you."*
>
> – Peter Sandeen, Marketing messaging specialist.

Taking a broader view, if selling a business is not your aim, the positives of growing a personal brand—even as a sideshow to the main carnival of a solid business—far outweigh the negatives. People like to do business with people they like and learn from, and that's never going to change.

Your LinkedIn Profile

There are probably few people in your industry ranking in the top 5% on LinkedIn, even though it's not that difficult to fix. You can find out what your LI influence is, too. Just log in to LinkedIn and type: www.linkedin.com/sales/ssi

Here's a secret: most solo professionals (who aren't brand strategists) have an influence rank that is abysmal. Happily, though, anyone can work on their influence relating to several factors:

people searching/connecting, sharing valuable insights, recommendations and relationship building.

Doing the easiest tasks first, you'll need to work on several elements in the profile, including images, about, and testimonies.

Engagement is two-way. Perhaps book into your weekly schedule around 15 minutes to check Notifications and comment on influential people's posts.

Brand Builder LinkedIn Tip:

You'll want to make sure your profile is visible to all. Just go to (Me) and click Settings & Privacy, then Visibility. Under profile discovery and visibility off LinkedIn, select 'yes'. Your profile then shows in a web search, which can be very handy for others if specifically looking for you. I also tick 'notify connections when you're in the news' – one can hope, can't one? And I allow mentions and tags.

Cover image: This is a background shot, best with a blank space in the middle and a book or speaker shot on the far right. (This is because mobile shifts the profile photo over). Make LinkedIn images in Canva or buy a customised design at the right size, which is generally about 1900 x 550 pixels, but check this.

Profile image: A professional head shot with a clear background is best.

About: This is the part which everyone goes to first, so make it great.

For the profile, read your LinkedIn page and your 'About us' page aloud to see where you can improve the text. Get out your who, what and why pitch. Work these key things in there:

- what my tribe wants to achieve – one line of insight into this
- 'claim to fame' – if a book writer or TED talker
- what problem I solve or knowledge of something that can help others
- experience and service I deliver (keep to what most people understand)
- what results I will deliver (or if in a career, what results the company delivers)
- my passionate reason for teaching or reaching others
- an action you want them to take or friendly, open invitation.

Write in the direct 'I' voice, rather than third person. We all know it's written by you, so claim it!

Writing it off-site, check if this will be under 2600 characters, which is the limit. Give it a grammar and spelling check, please! If you respect your words, hire an editor to check that the About and Experience reads well. Remember, it is your profile reflective of your public-facing self... don't let it be vague or rusty or non-existent.

Here's a brief, fictional 'About me' example:

At 13, I wanted more than anything to be a singer. After a career in theatre arts instruction, I now help novice singers and speechmakers *project their beautiful voice.* My speaker clients have gone from barely talking loudly enough to be heard 6 feet away, to going on stage in front of 500 people and projecting their voice right to the back.

Working with clients led to me determining the *four steps to vocal success.* An introduction to this in video form (link in publications) is available to anyone curious about better speaking.

Breaking this down, this bio included: her personal motivation, her main career choice, how she helps her target group now, and a specific outcome from working with her. Then what format or model she uses to create the results. Plus the soft call to action for those now curious.

Headline. Once your book is in circulation, you can add 'author' to your headline on LinkedIn. Don't be too showy though. It's cringy to put headlines like: The Best Speaker on Selling Skills, or 'I show you how to use LinkedIn to get clients' – that is just boring. Be specific and keep it real.

If, say, you use a word like 'equine', also use the word 'horse' elsewhere, liberally, so people searching for such an expert with the layman's word will find you.

Company page. You can set up a company page and upload a square jpeg of either your book (if an author) or logo, then go back to your personal profile to edit it, search for the company page, select it and wallah! An image appears next to your company or author name.

Remember, you can't form a connection with a browser of your profile if they can't first understand what you do. Keep all the terms simple, relate it to common ground, and use your conversational voice.

Skills. You can add 40 skills and you can rearrange them in priority order, ready to be endorsed. Go to *Me: View Profile*, scroll to Skills. Add + (or pencil to edit). Click ... to re-order your skills.

If you put your profile in Creator mode, you add in the three to five subjects that you talk about and these show up as hashtags. Make sure you use the relevant one or two of those hashtags when posting an update about your area.

It's actually quite easy to have a solid personal brand on LinkedIn, it's just that most people don't want to do these little things.

Email Tip

An email signature leaves a lasting impression on people, so make sure it includes the name of your books or show, your area and phone numbers, and logo if desired. This should be a tiny file and can include your head shot too, as people remember faces more than names. I know it looks naff to you, but it leaves a personable impression.

Even if using Gmail or similar, you can set up signatures. In the settings (gear icon) signatures is under General. If you're on the mobile, signatures are not generally included unless you take the step of adding it, so remember that your emails may look at little on-the-fly.

8.

The Author's Website and Content

Author or Speaker Websites are an important aspect to build a foundation to promote online. The first consideration is obvious.

Do you want it to be uniquely personal... or primarily business?

Whether a 'personal name' or a 'business name' website, you should showcase your own products, offerings, courses, and community memberships. If you have specific knowledge or have compiled several people's real stories into one theme, then why not turn them into eBooks, books, or video interviews.

Business name websites can be sold to someone else, so that's something to consider as well. Promoted as an individual topic area, these will attract a wider array of people who want to know about the topic rather than specifically what you say.

Your leadership (e.g. running a solid blog and writing a book, eBook or podcast) helps your business to gain clients and advocates. That is, as long as it relates to the theme of your niche information.

Some great examples of a personal brand, built online, are:

AliBrown.com – mentor to entrepreneur women

Nickbowditch.com - storytelling expert, authentic speaker

GregSavage.com.au – recruitment industry leader

In these sites, you'll find a great variety of personal styles. Looking closely, you'll notice that a perfect look and feel is not the most important aspect. Clarity of message and being authentically themselves is arguably the calling cards of these experts.

Choosing the Right Website Platform and Design

You can do many things without forking out $2,500+ in design costs and without being a coding genius. Sure, there are designers who specialise in author website design and these designers charge from $1,000-$1,500 for a complete design that matches brand (1 long scrolling page or 5 individual pages), and that is fine to help, providing it's a CMS where you can get into it. Jin&Co is one of these designers.

A CMS is a *Content Management System*: a way to take charge of your content edits and blog posting. However, it comes with undue responsibilities, like blocking spam, blocking hackers, running backups, updating theme and core, and compressing images. Plugins are seemingly simple... but running many of them without conflict and crashes is not.

If you want to go straight into using a personal domain (e.g. Jenny-Lee.com.au) but don't want the hassles of hosting, CPanel, threat security, or maintaining plugins and a theme, then Squarespace or Ghost (ghost.org) is your best bet. (Note: Ghost can be set up on a different virtual server, but it's easier to use Ghost Pro managed hosting).

Ghost is an open-source platform that's really fast. With a wide range of templates, capacity of up to 1,000 members and 2 staff, you would pay US$25 per month. Or start with the solo plan for US$15 per month, which also allows 1,000 members. Members can log in and you could later charge them monthly fees for fresh content.

Just a final note, Ghost platform is run as a non-profit organisation. Some of the features: it has built-in SEO control, built-in security, and you own your data. Downside: each website needs a new Ghost subscription.

With *Squarespace*, once you grab a template and pay a moderate fee of around AU$25 per month, you can access many free videos to learn the SquareSpace page builder. Don't forget to add a subscriber opt-in form, with a juicy freebie.

Your website will need an SSL certificate and this should come with the platform or hosting and not be a separate charge. However, someone techy might need to help your website use the HTTPS properly (once off).

Just to compare with how 60% of us run WordPress software and choose a host, let's do the numbers. For my website hosting I pay US$10 per site per month (x 3), then for course platform and lead software, Thrive Themes Suite (AU$40 p.m.), developer fees when code needs tweaking, and Askimet anti-spam. Updraft is a security plugin option that is free, but then there are domain name security options to consider, and domain redirects. It all adds up!

In contrast, with hosted website platforms, you don't pay extra for page builders, plugins or hosting. You would have plenty of budget leftover for some customised book/course cover graphics, lead magnet image, and banners that really pop.

Your branded website needs strong visuals. Here, it pays to find a branding-oriented graphic designer.

You will start by thinking of a theme and relaying what mood/ values you want to convey. Then, they will choose two to three appropriate colours, fonts, imagery. Quite possibly, you will add a tagline that goes with the theme. You may even have had a visual model done for a signature program and use this colour set.

First, you need a professional, smiling headshot. This is not taken in your kitchen, with the cat, at your wedding, or with a drink in hand. It is taken by a professional head shot photographer, as mentioned. Get several types of shots with varied aspect ratios because they come in very handy in all your media uses.

We need a banner for the top of the website, but some of us should not attempt to design our own banners! Instead, you could order a beautified author banner in the various sizes required by YouTube, LinkedIn, FB and your website, at a cost of around $75 from Fiverr, saving you much time and frustration.

While size will change to suit the platform, these banners should look consistent across the web. Your logo is more a square or rectangle but any banner (for website) is extra wide and only say 150–200 pixels high. These are not the same thing!

A banner has a background which works in with the name and does not overshadow it. Illustrator designers can do cool fades of your smiling photo into the background, which in their parlance is called *blur with background transparency*.

Hard to believe, but Google ranking and reputation is affected by brand. The popularity of your brand name is arguably more important in terms of rankings than backlinks these days.

Reputable backlinks to the website used to be how the popularity of a website was demonstrated to Google. When speaking about the spread of disinformation on the Internet in 2008, Google's ex-CEO and Chairman said:

> *Brands are the solution, not the problem.*
> *Brands are how you sort out the cesspool.*
> *- Eric Schmidt*

In addition to your new content targeted at your market, your brand [or real name] must be on everyone's lips – I mean fingertips!

Facing the About Us Page with Courage

Many business owners/consultants chicken out when tasked with the challenge of writing a distinctive About Us page. In fact, many have been known to omit all traces of a person behind a business and allude to years of experience as if a ghost runs the company.

If that's you, don't do this! Always put your name and team names in the About page; be honest about experience and values. You can also include prior business-related experiences, even if it's not the same business type, if it tells the story of your integrity and results focus.

After all, we relate to people and their personal values far more than is usually recognised. We tend to look for similarity in values, as well as a smidgen of empathy and proof of customer results.

Not only that, also include personality in the copy. Any copywriter you brief should have an idea of what your personality is like, what common things you often advise clients (pearls of wisdom), as well as the facts about why and how the business started.

This makes for a well-rounded picture of the person behind the service or product.

Using my face, not some model's, helps others connect with a real person

Create, Don't Copy Your Content

You don't need to copy other people for your social media imagery and postings, just free your creative side.

Don't fret, there is an easier way to do this! It's best to use pro-level *templates* to create all different images based on your topic theme, brand colours, and the aims for the pieces.

With regular content, there are three key aims:

1. To inspire someone

2. To educate someone

3. To give yourself authority in the space

Creative content can apply to posters, infographics, bookmark design, videos, a helpful, informative website, or custom software, e.g., Simply Budgets. I made a rudimentary hourly rate calculator for freelancers, using Excel, and offered it as a *freebie* to blog readers. It had a higher opt-in rate than all other free guides I ever offered, of 11%.

Blog:

Curating reviews on the best technology solutions, the best books, how to use something, or commenting on trending news for your industry has the effect of aligning yourself to the industry and garnering lots of views.

What the heck are you doing on the socials?

It's time to contemplate your current actions.

- What do you post on social media – is it planned?

- Does it represent your ethos and creative content?

- Is some of it personal story and the rest education?

- Are you reading 'thought leader' articles, watching TED talks and doing short courses to keep pace with change and inform your writing?

- Are you thinking about how your business and its publications can adapt and solve one or two of the current problems you see in your niche?

Rather than repeating trite quotes and reposting cat videos, these actions can help with creating a personal brand that's *right on the money*.

'Right on the money' is at the intersection of:

- What a good chunk of people are desiring now, e.g. a stable income, a happy and peaceful home life, beautiful art customised to them, magical de-cluttering, etc.

- What you/your team can offer up the ideal solution for, along the track.

- What represents your values and your personal creed.

Visual marketing

We'd be wise to express our personal brand on social media. *Canva Pro* is an online tool that helps us create some brilliant little designs for social media. Having pre-filled templates at the right sizes for social media or blog, and with thousands of video or photo stock to select among, it may save soloists a lot of content creation time.

However, be careful that you don't just buy yourself a job. Virtual assistants can use these designer tools for you, perhaps with a keen eye for *design balance* and a consistent look from the start. Another idea is to get your colour-matched photography and visual branding/logos done right by a designer, then use this as a base for all your social postings.

Tip! To keep things consistent, add your brand colours and fonts if you get the paid version of Canva. This Brand Kit saves your colours (HEX numbers for online) and logos. Inserting your own images into templates keeps your uniqueness alive.

Sometimes, just playing with Canva can help you get started in using visual imagery to help your everyday marketing. They give you fancy elements, sized templates for every occasion, and now they offer printing at great prices too. Along with other edit tools, Canva can remove the background of a photo, leaving your image to stand out on a vibrant colour block.

Other creative apps to help you include:

Quotefancy.com: get ready-made quote images for famous quotes, sorted by type.

Picmonkey.com: edit and 'filter' your own photos, for free.

HubSpot Blog ideas generator (https://www.hubspot.com/blog-topic-generator?): five headline ideas for free, pay for 250.

Autogramtags.com: get automatic hashtags for Instagram or Facebook.

App.Biteable.com: Biteable gives various templates for DIY video animations. Good for making 30-second book trailers in your theme colours. Pay $US19 and you can download a final video for commercial use.

Descript.com: a new video and audio editor, Descript takes your script and with some help from you, makes natty videos for YouTube or TikTok. Your videos can be edited (remove umms) and output with automatic transcription, although some learning is required. Podcasters can use it for editing sound and implanting music. (US$15 p.m.)

———

How to Publish on Social Media

First, decide on your likeliest social media channels and regularity of posting. More creative is better than more often.

When you make short videos, don't forget that it's best to upload each directly to Facebook or LinkedIn, to get the most views.

In addition, if you want to get started with LinkedIn content creation, it's wise to not put your website links in each post. Put a couple paragraphs of text, optional picture, or video (with subtitles) but if you put links, LinkedIn doesn't show it to many of your connections at all. These platforms do not want patrons leaving too often! The exception is links to your LinkedIn based long articles (or 'newsletter').

On Facebook, save time by using the scheduler for your page to post two weeks' worth of content at one sitting. Remember, your author or consultant page should be a business page, complete with beautiful cover shot.

When creating these posts, do it in Meta Business Suite's *Planner*, where you can 'Schedule' to choose the day and time.

You can also make a slide-show from still images inside the Planner. If you have Canva Pro, the simple Content Calendar allows for scheduled posting to all your other social platforms in one go, without downloading.

———

Are you picking up a creative content mindset yet? I hope so. It's a great way to get wider attraction on social media, free, while also reaffirming all that your personal brand stands for.

So, no more worrying over what to do… Pick up your keyboard, drawing tablet or favourite video app, and create a simple brand awareness campaign.

Marketing Gravy Trains

According to Jennifer at Power of Words,
copywriter/editor

The early '90s

Money poured into Print marketing, TV ads, Direct mail, radio ads and editorials. So owners of mass media got rich. Hello, Murdoch?

Late '90s/early 2000s

With uptake of the Internet, companies flocked to online marketing - splash-page websites, emails, long sales letters, and copywriters wrote white papers (PDFs) to give away. 'Permission Marketing' by Seth Godin came out. My 1st eBook started to sell online.

2006: The Gravy Train begins

Companies knew they needed a website, and that they needed to rank on Google, so this started the SEO and web development gravy train.
In 2009-14, I wrote copy and blog posts for small businesses.

2012-15: Content Marketing ramps up

Wahoo! Freelancers turned into agencies to pitch for content creation and content marketing. The ability to write variants of copy for different social media (and design graphics) was--and still is--sought.

9.

Forming Partnerships

Partnering with other relevant specialists will help your reach. If you don't yet have a big email list, then partner with someone who is selling to the same people and does have a list. If you become known for one thing, this will help attract the right partners to help with the promotional aspect.

Even if it's sharing to their audience about a latest release for a cool resource, this kind of thing often gets results. If the partner recommends it, then their followers' trust will flow on down to you.

Virtual book tours involve taking your message to several bloggers you've struck up a friendship with, one after the other, for a condensed period. You might also do a Review Swap with other author-bloggers. This placement would mainly be for the editorial section or your own website and not for an Amazon customer review (as it is against their strict Terms).

Sites for locating these authors are Goodreads author groups, Facebook author groups, and individual book blogger sites.

Try these:

https://www.bookbloggersaustralia.com.au/ Search under genre, then ask for reviews to those relevant.

https://australianauthors.net.au/australian-authors/ Get a free book listing

https://www.collabosaurus.com
If marketing a product, you can collaborate officially with others (from bakers to clothing makers to photographers) and those with similar reach. Hint: think of your course as a product. Take a tour, browse opportunities, then create your own listing, supply some nice photos and details. Upgrade for more interest.

If you don't ask influencers or associates, your promotions won't get anywhere!

Grow through Affiliates/Partners

Once you've got banners made, a website, some mottos, mini posters and even promo codes, you could recruit affiliates for your system and book. This is a step for the advanced marketing person and you normally need some pre-written email copy all ready to intrigue their email subscribers.

Simply, if you can't think of what to do for promotions besides blasting Facebook groups with book covers, then you're not really trying! Off-line media, magazines and relationship partnering can get your book some free publicity.

Partnering or asking contacts has helped me by:

a) getting me free press coverage in local street magazines

b) getting a massive number of hits to my freelance business book page through saying yes to an Intuit freelance tools blog campaign

c) interesting 200 new US email subscribers through offering a mini course as part of an Infostack $49 package deal.

For exchange partnerships, blogging is a great idea. I've often invited another author to guest interview on my blog and we share the final post on LinkedIn, Twitter and elsewhere to gain traction.

How To:

When writing blog articles in the You voice or I voice, use personal expressions and colloquial language. You then copy & paste the first intriguing (hook) paragraph to your social media update to help people gain interest. Without expressly putting the link, you might allude to the related hyperlink in your profiles so that people can find it.

10.

How to Change Your Positioning

Don't look, I'm changing my positioning!

Some people don't think of themselves as a 'brand', let alone something to position. Before we do any brand re-positioning, we need to delve into our ideal avatars, what our service or program does for people, in other words RESULTS, and what level these ideal people are at in their learning journey. This all dictates what level you will play at and what you will charge.

When I was setting up Power of Words services, I did a lot of SWOT research, mostly to discover indirect threats and potential opportunities. Whenever considering a new book or membership or service, out I go to Facebook groups to see what businesspeople are struggling with. 'Lurking' (with good intent) has become a sport, but asking specific questions in authority groups is even better.

Authority groups are usually groups made up of a mix of business coaches, publicity agents, authors, trainers, etc, and not your average hobbyist. It's best if they're based in your country.

Sometimes though, the level we will play at is dictated by our confidence, our networking, and our own skill base. Purely for planning, it helps to know *who* you can reach in advance of a personal brand story and book launch. For one thing, it enables you to order the right amount and right type of wine/coffee and cheese!

A problem I've noticed is intending book authors don't have a clear audience that tomorrow they could ask a question of and get a valid survey response. Everything is fuzzily pictured in some rosy future when they have the audience. So, making this audience crystal clear and picking them out from your network is your next step.

Who Can You Reach?

It makes sense to align with what people in your circles are looking for... and the kind of person you are. Take a look at your own blog content, mastermind events, or talks—did you connect with the audience? What kind of businesses did they have, or were they studying or working and interested in starting a business? Were they experienced freelancers? Mums with skills who want an extra income?

The thing is, if you pitch at the wrong crowd or at the wrong level, your talks and information products will fall flat. Talking to retired artists about corporate life and burnout? Not the right fit.

It soon came clear that people reading my blog were not looking for 'executive level' info; far more often, they were looking for how to make their new authorship or services a success. I gleaned this by examining website visitor movements to see what Australians were reading and by a few comments on posts. Most would read the basic posts about writing and publishing a book. Other topics were for the advanced but still got hits. 'Creating a media kit' was more likely to be read by the already-published author.

Sharing some useful techniques in their area of desire will thus be far more effective than shooting straight for the top (C-suite level) when it comes to brand positioning.

I met a cartoonist at an event who had talent but lacked a strategy. The discussion we had was about how, as a commission-based cartoonist, he found it hard to pick a winning book and make enough commissions. That was his only paradigm. I pointed out that if he niched his cartooning and spoke only to people in that niche, he was likely to be able to command a worthy fee, like others I knew of.

LinkedIn Tips

For many in a company, they must enhance their personal brand on LinkedIn first. So commit to filling in all the elements, including a background wide banner that intrigues in what you do.

There is also posting relevant content, and did you know you can become a 'content creator' on LinkedIn, with a special topic set (#)? This turns your 'connect' button into a 'follow' button.

It's ideal to put up two or three special Featured pages. These 'featured' items can be awesome presentations or brief articles. You can even insert a very short video at the top of your profile next to your photo. (It's all under 'Edit Profile').

Some executives also get a speaker reel made, called a showreel. This is high-level videography of you speaking, and I'm told it is key to getting more conference public speaking opportunities.

After you change your personal brand position:

- tweak your LinkedIn profile 'about' section and headline with a keyword of your topic area
- ensure that you explain what value *you* bring, not just your organisation's usual words
- add some better subject areas people can endorse
- add your "Publications", e.g. books, eBooks, or slideshows
- put in a unique background cover image that has your brand colours, slogan, book cover
- consider changing your profile to Creator Mode, with topics you'll post about.

While you're there, it's a good idea to do searches through 2nd connections for key people who are writing or speaking in your industry and in your niche. This is to remain aware of what others are doing, without copying them or thinking you fall short.

Only recently I realised the true power of connecting on LinkedIn.

All those events you've been to and met people at—did you keep their business card? If it was fairly recent, get the card out and type the name into LinkedIn. Write a friendly greeting to go with the connection request, reminding them where they met you. Then, offer to help by sharing a relevant article, endorsing a skill of theirs, offering a referral from a friend, reviewing a book of theirs, etc.

When it comes time to launch your own book or course, imagine how many people you can then turn to and ask to jump on board and pre-read, give an endorsement, or buy your book at a great price. It's not such a big favour to ask then.

This is so much better than just paying for book ads and hoping and praying. Because people do business with (and buy books from) *people they like*, ensure that when you change your brand positioning, you bring those in your network closer to you.

That means being real. Think of Michael Hyatt and his immensely popular blog and videos. Does he talk to you like a real person? Yes. Does he stand for something? Yes, he stands for offering useful advice for authors and being clear about the value of doing something. Not shouting from the roof-tops the name of his last book. Same with Romney Nelson, a publishing trainer and seller of 30,000 books.

Positioning a personal brand takes some forethought and align-ment, of thinking what people in your sphere will value. It's most definitely not about your pricing. Like Andrew Griffiths titled a book, *Someone has to be the most expensive, why not you?*

11.

Turning your Brand into an Income Stream

Every day I get an offer via Facebook ads for a new way to turn my persona and expertise into an income, usually a promised $100K a year. I often have a look at offer or what they say, but I am not one to just jump on a gravy train without thinking it through. These are just some ways to gain income if you don't like regular writing.

Make 'your community' content area. Turn your knowledge into a video-containing app and advertise levels of membership. This is easiest with Ghost, the helpful publishing platform that allows memberships. (It helps to have a following I should think, but certainly saves some time in technical work). See **https:// ghost.org**.

Another nice way to facilitate a paid community is through creating a course on your own name website. I've done this via Thrive Apprentice, which works with WordPress (the .org kind) and allows internal student comments. True community interaction will need to be somewhere else. Membership sites can be next-level hard to get going, as I found out during my MemberPress days.

Take PLR (private label rights) eBooks or course materials and make it your own, reselling the same stuff other people have. (Originality is lacking here, but I suppose it's good for those who want to have something to offer without figuring out what).

Gain a million followers on Instagram or YouTube through sharing how-to or hack videos and aligning with other content creators. (As long as the content of the videos aligns perfectly with your intended message and you have a plan to monetise this). This is a lot harder than most think.

Bring people the message with a podcast. Interviewing influential others in a field is a good way of getting some of that sunshine too. If you've something new to say on a subject, then a podcast is certainly made easier these days. All you need is a good microphone, an editing app (or editor), and subscription to a distribution feed. Two people hosting a podcast makes a nice harmony and allows for double the marketing. How you monetise it is, after gaining a following, to offer a sponsorship ($30-70 CPM) or have a call-to-action to your masterclass, mastermind, or course.

Make a high-level course. People with a personal brand and well-known expertise are getting on the online teaching bandwagon. Creators (60,000 to date) have earned around $5 billion collectively using Kajabi, a number that has doubled since 2021.

So, what do these course platforms offer?

All-in-one platform **Kajabi** has a new AI creator studio, which helps trainers create video scripts, course outlines, landing pages, sales emails, etc. It seems to have the best suite of engagement & sales tools, which is why it's more expensive than other platforms, sitting at US$149 per month at its base level.

Thinkific is focused on course building and offers plans that are US$69, $99 and $199 per month, but the lower level does not offer bulk emailing all students, which is a nuisance.

Skool is a newcomer. It's a bit different in that's based on engaging a niche community, where you offer simple free courses. However, they've now introduced a paid course option. The platform, after trial, costs US$99 per month. Influencers and coaches tend to like this one.

If you're starting out, it's best to keep costs down when making a course. Simple training presentations can be recorded with Canva templates and a talking head video voiceover, although this is not high resolution. Alternatively, use a PowerPoint template with their voiceover function, exported to movie format. This becomes a giant file you need to compress before uploading to a course platform.

You may also need a video editing tool for other types of videos.

～

Basically, there are hundreds of ways to build a valued community and make some money, however there are many unforeseen hurdles to overcome. For instance, are you adept at the type of media you'll be working with? This could be talking on camera (smiling and having energy), turning someone's bland words into something your very own, or working out how to advertise your amazing products with social ads without going broke (no joke!).

People will start to willingly hand over their money when you reach the point of having plentiful content that authentically talks to their own desires. Even if you don't mention the emotional side and the desires, if the outcomes and benefits you talk about are what they really want, bingo, you can create value and make some sales. The benefit message has to be clear most of all.

Many people get stuck on the tech. So start with your skills and aims, not with the technology advertised as the perfect solution. Roughly map out your angle, hook and niche audience before starting with an expensive software program. Remember that it's you and your knowledge they're coming for, not a pretty looking page.

Creating a Course or Program that Makes Profits, not Tired Eyes

Start with looking at two of your specific niches on Google Trends. Look at which of the two is rising or higher in your country.

The topic really doesn't have to be anything to do with business, but what it must do is:

- Help a particular group learn something really important to them
- Share in the area you know the most about and like to talk/write about
- Meet a demand already there (perhaps there are similar things overseas). In this case, try to talk to strangers with a survey or poll or in a Facebook group.

Advertising is all part of creating an online course or member program. Don't even think about trying to organically rank in Google for a specific niche in the first three months, unless you have 10 or 20 hours spare per week to do so.

You'll need one Facebook business account (business suite) and Facebook group. It might be easier for you to run a public group at first and create a small private group once you have course attendees. Ensure that this activity doesn't burn up all your time.

Put your face and brief authentic story on the landing page of the online course.

Make sure that they can finish the course within three months and it's also got some depth to enable a learning curve and promised outcome. This is not a hack you're selling.

Videos and audio formats have more value and they enable visual or aural learning, which a lot of people really love.

Don't spend lots of time stuck on how best to set this up. Instead, you could get a course design expert to develop the course/program website design for around $1,000-$1,500. You'll want to move ahead quickly but you don't want lots of extra problems with it, so it's important your course developer is really trustworthy.

If you've time to learn how, it's not that difficult. The large course platform providers like *Thinkific* provide training and are fairly easy to navigate. It's also designed to take you through the initial steps to coming up with audience problems and a basic structure.

For a deeper dive, see my workbook, *'The Mega Book and Course Planner'*. As well as prompts, it contains all the good research resources found on my five-year journey into memberships and course development.

Use a webinar to promote it

If you want something to offer people in order to instill trust and get more people interested, you can run a WIIFM webinar: 'what's in it for me' style. A title with a must-have outcome is good for your informational webinar. Done well, this style helps you to be credible in their eyes and ready to buy your online course or program. This is ideal to be advertised.

Perhaps start off with how you got started and all the bumps and dollars spent along the way. The webinar should contain some great tips and examples in your niche, the inside track, and be about 40 minutes to 1.5 hours long.

If not a webinar, then some gurus say a video series can work well, and it is easy to put an action-taker button underneath the final video on the page for them to buy the course or program.

Whichever way you choose, remember to appeal to their emotions first. This might be fear of being in the spotlight, stuttering on stage, or doubts about starting a business. Acknowledge their fear, give the emotion acceptance, and say how you moved beyond it. This is far better than trying to appear perfect anyway.

If you're selling training and development, perhaps mention how you went on a learning path as well (formal learning or in-person seminars) and what it showed you. You can't very well be a teacher without being a student first.

What should you charge for the online program?

If it's all online, those who are pros at this say price the program about $500 to $2,000, once validated. At the upper end, the person may expect some physical materials, like a workbook and tech tutorial, and monthly group coaching sessions with Q&As. You could throw in your new book and a private Facebook group where they can get answers and join similar others in the quest. People learning love to have similar company for support.

The bonuses are a way to increase the package value without it actually being anything customised every time.

That said, some coaches like to include a free individual session with them, which is a seeming bargain when packaged in with a training program. So, have a think about what is the time commitment for you. Also consider whether they are more likely to be

DIY learners on a budget or are likely to pay more to get personalised coaching sessions. Conversations with lots of prospects are where we learn these things.

If you run any kind of support agency, inevitably you'll get enquiries for having your team do it. This is because people hate to struggle on alone if they have the money to pay. It's amazing how their budget goes up when faced with a technology block or having to do social media posts every day!

Complementary Sales

A lot of newer bloggers and authors try to make a few indirect sales, such as through affiliate products or advertising.

But, until you reach the approximate level of 10,000 engaged followers or 2,000+ unique visitors a month, this could well be a hit and miss affair. One that pays about enough for the family cat to eat.

Some advertising programs rely on big followings and only want influencers. Canva recently changed to only allow social influencers to be an affiliate, recognising their power to sell.

Once you have written a book, start thinking about some complementary sales for it. You may have a freebie that gets new visitor interest, but a workbook or journal or online course might be just the ticket for making more out of a mighty book launch.

This workbook can be paid digital download or a printable copy.

The Audacious Agency offer both: *the Most Audacious Marketing Planner* allows one year of jotting your content goals, thoughts, achievements, and project lists. It comes with bonus videos.

This kind of product helps the new community member, makes them warm to you, and is a $12 – $30 offering that most can afford.

To create this, browse through templates (try Creative Market) or hire a graphic designer to take your ideas and make it into a nicely designed workbook.

Never forget to offer this as an easy low-cost option whenever you give a talk or interview. People love a shortcut and tailored guidance when planning goals.

Jennifer Lancaster

12.

Shine in Your Introduction Pitch

I've been to a lot of networking groups. As an observer of words, I find it interesting what people say in their 60-second pitch. A saleslady at a local group said something like, "Men and women are talking about anti-ageing and I help you discover how to prevent anti-ageing". She had said the opposite of what she meant.

People who go to network marketing events tend to pick up certain lines and re-use them, and soon enough, you've heard them before. Even worse, they are very generic. GENERIC is the kiss of death in relating to people.

Do you know what people like and relate to? Is it a pitch they've heard before or is it authentic and uniquely you? Is it an image that forms in their minds and stays?

Can you also spin it around from "I am a… or I can do….. to: "I've done this for clients (achievement) and now I show others how to do this too, even if they don't know where to start."

To build credibility within a room in a short time… you've got to walk your talk. Smile, be confident. Don't speak in a monotone (observe the news reporters' voices). Enjoy what you're saying. If you make a fluff, laugh about it and correct.

If you can get your pitch right and are a leader in your micro-niche, then you will be ready for media interviews. Interviews allow you to expand from your initial pitch to them… to why your message is important for the public to know.

Let's use an example of a mundane, practical business: Roofing. Not normally a thriller? What about if a roofer with 25 years' experience told you that more than half of all roof companies overcharge asbestos roof customers (just an example). They very well could – that's beside the point – the main thing here is to research a fact that's quite shocking.

Without naming names, as an expert you do have the right to expose bad practices in your industry. The fact is, people are generally looking for a genuine deal, a helpful service, and <u>truth always costs less and creates more interest</u>.

Why do I say that?

When you tell the unvarnished truth in your introductory pitch or in your content online, you spark interest in people. Not many are game enough to say controversial things or be a lone wolf – but if you check out your facts, stay legal and do so – I believe you'll find it costs you less than hyping or mimicking your message.

It creates more interest because the authentic, single-minded message of hope, of freedom, or of truth, creates a kind of gravitational pull. Here's what Mark Bonchek wrote at Harvard Business Review:

> To create a force of attraction, you have to
> go beyond thinking about value propositions
> and target audiences. Gravity originates in
> a *shared purpose* that is created *with* your
> stakeholders as co-creators, not
> just *to* or *for* them as consumers.

Messaging: Be Iconic

Giving something as hard to pin down as 'marketing messages' a name like 'icons' gives it an anchor. *Iconic* is both the name of a book by Scott McKain and a technique to iconise your brand messaging and become distinctive.

Down to brass tacks, it is repeating a stand-out point in all forms of promotion (or even on the phone). An example message is, *in book publishing, finding the correct reader avatar is important, because people don't just buy one book on the subject; they buy a bookshelf full.* 'They don't just book one book on the subject, they buy a bookshelf full' is a stand-out point.

This technique is taking something little known and showcasing it.

Another one might be your made-up phrase that has harmony,

like: 'niche marketing is the answer to your nightly prayers for your business'. Answer to your nightly prayers = something that sets off the imagination.

Not about just cute phrasing, this glint of brilliance shines from the iceberg of truth. The rest is hidden, but soon to be revealed to the new client in the form of lead magnets (e.g. subscriber reports, guides, tools, videos) and the way your business puts that statement into action.

Personalities have the dexterity in this that big companies don't. You could discover brilliant new marketing messages just by listening and talking to potential customers. Listen to the clichés and the sweeping statements too – even these can be a clue to the distinctive marketing message you will create.

Making these messages correspond to the actual distinction in your brand is the key. The brand *Thank You* may have a charitable *why* but they also deliver the products in ways that match their own company objectives. Less packaging, books where you choose the price, creative and viral videos, etc.

The way you do things is as important as the why.

Here are some examples. Don't put 'sustainable paper' on letters to notify clients when you could email. Don't rubbish another firm's approach – this will just reflect badly on you. Don't put out workshop flyers on flimsy strips of inkjet-printed paper; it's cheap but says you're cheap too.

Conclusion

Many soloists start out looking at others for inspiring their brand and messaging, which may inadvertently lead them to appear just like 90% of others in the space: buzz-word lovers, generic or broad, and struggling to attract.

So, the most important thing to remember about personalising your brand and making it consistent is to plan it! Take a day out to look at what is said on your website or LinkedIn, what kind of offers you might have, how your quality comes across in your marketing collateral, and match this with the plan to emphasise your personal values and strengths.

Remember, everything with your name attached reflects your personal brand, whether you create books or run the books. An author page banner on Facebook is all part of your online brand presence. The suit or outfit worn to your talks is part of your personal brand.

If you're yet to start with online presence-building, then doing the exercises in this book will help you get really clear on what you represent to your market and the overarching message.

Don't know where to start marketing? Then go and poll those you're targeting to find out preferred media habits. After all, your target market may not hang out on Instagram, so before you spend 500 hours on making this your shop window, think about the busy and distracted ideal client or reader and how you could attract and interest them.

Being courageous in revealing your background and learning journey will pay dividends for personal services people, while other professionals may like to focus on why they specifically do this role. In the webinars, conversations or lives, also create a picture of a solid future for clientele.

Don't be like other apples, be uncom-pear-able... Authentically yourself!

Learn More

The Mega Book & Course Planning Workbook
https://JenniferLancaster.com.au/books/
mega-book-and-course-planning-workbook.

Free! *More Author Revenue* course
https://jenniferlancaster.com.au/courses/
more-author-revenue/

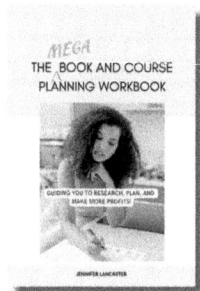

Book Creation Success course (plus self-publishing tutorials)
https://bookcreationsuccess.thinkific.com/

Free 25-minute author consultation:
https://bookjenniferlancaster.as.me/

Resources:

Canva – Design School. https://www.canva.com/designschool/

Descript.com – Video editor and transcriber.

GetResponse – Lessons on Email Marketing and a great EMS. https://www.getresponse.com/resources

Ubersuggest – Tools and information on search and keyword research. https://NeilPatel.com/ubersuggest

Zoho Social – Cheaper Social Media Management. https://www.zoho.com/social/

Social Follow and Learn:

Contribute on Quora Space. https://theauthorexpert.quora.com/

YouTube: https://www.youtube.com/@businessauthoracademy

Indie Author Blog: https://www.jenniferlancaster.com.au/blog

References:

1. Mark Boncheck, Harvard Business Review. 'A Good Digital Strategy Creates a Gravitational Pull', 2017. https://hbr.org/2013/03/purpose-is-good-shared-purpose. Accessed 2023.

2. Brendon Burchard, 'High Performance Habits', 2017. High Performance Research LLC. P.198

Jennifer Lancaster